CLEVELAND A to Z

An Essential Compendium for Visitors and Residents Alike

BLACK SQUIRREL BOOKS® 🐿®

Frisky, industrious black squirrels are a familiar sight on the Kent State University campus and the inspiration for Black Squirrel Books®, a trade imprint of The Kent State University Press, Kent, Ohio. www.KentStateUniversityPress.com

Published in 2019 by Black Squirrel Books®, Kent, Ohio
First published in 2017 by the Western Reserve Historical Society.
Copyright © 2017 by the Western Reserve Historical Society
All rights reserved

ISBN 978-1-60635-390-5
Manufactured in Korea

No part of this book may be used or reproduced, in any manner whatsoever, without written permission from the Publisher, except in the case of short quotations in critical reviews or articles.

Images: Unless noted otherwise, all historical images are from the collections of the Western Reserve Historical Society. All contemporary images are courtesy of Lauren R. Pacini.

Design by Timothy Lachina
Walter Greene+Co.

Cataloging information is available at the Library of Congress.

23 22 21 20 19   5 4 3 2 1

FOR DLE, DVT, NK, WDM…THE PAST IS ALWAYS PRESENT

Cleveland A to Z celebrates the 150th Anniversary of the Western Reserve Historical Society.

CLEVELAND A to Z

An Essential Compendium for Visitors and Residents Alike

John J. Grabowski **Contemporary Photography by Lauren R. Pacini**

Black Squirrel Books® Kent, Ohio

"I love Cleveland and its eccentrically screwy and strangely American splendor."

Anthony Bourdain, chef, author

Moses Cleaveland (1754–1806)

TABLE OF CONTENTS

Foreword	ix
Preface	xiii
Acknowledgments	xiv
Introduction	xvi
Agora	1
Alsbacher, Moses	2
Andrews's Folly	3
Birdtown	4
Boiardi, Hector (Ettore)	5
The Bridge War	6
Burning River	7
Cedar Avenue	8
Christmas Stories	9
Cleaveland, Moses	10
Cleveland Cultural Gardens	11
The Cleveland Orchestra	12
Cuyahoga River	13
Doan Brook	14
Downtown	15
Emerald Necklace	16
Erie	17
Euclid	18
Euclid Beach	19
The Flats	20
Franklin Castle	21
Garlick, Theodatus	22
Giddings Avenue	23
Glenville	24
Hanna, Marcus Alonzo	25
The Harvard Club	26
The Heights	27
Hessler	28
I-X Center	29
Joc-O-Sot	30
Johnson, Tom L.	31
Karamu House	32
Kingsbury Run	33
Kossuth Statue	34
Lake Views	35
League Park	36
Little Italy	37
The Mall	38
Moondog Coronation Ball	39
Morgan, Garrett	40
Mustard	41
Ness, Eliot	42
Ohio City	43
Owens, Jesse	44
Parma	45
Peerless	46
The Perils of Society	47
Perkins, Anna	48
Pierogies	49
Pittsburgh	50
Polka	51
Public Square	52
Quayle, Thomas	53
Rockefeller, John D.	54
Shaker Heights	55
Sherwin, Belle	56
The Shoreway	57
Short Vincent Street	58
Slavic Village	59
SOM Center Road	60
Stokes	61
Time Magazine	62
University Circle	63
The "Vans"	64
Vinegar Hill	65
Wade	66
Western Reserve/ Connecticut Western Reserve	67
Whiskey Island	68
X	69
Yellow Cab Company	70
Young, Cy	71
The Zoo	72
Index	74
Photo Gallery for Contemporary Images	80

FOREWORD
BY ROBERT H. JACKSON

"I love the normalcy of Cleveland. There are regular people there."

Drew Carey, comedian and TV host

There is a lot of crazy love out there for Cleveland. People love Cleveland's buildings, its culture, and its history. They love the huge trees that shade almost all of its neighborhoods, the storms that roll in off the lake, and the noise, flames, and odors that still rise from its factories and steel mills. If people have been seriously ill and gotten well again, they love Cleveland's medical centers. If they like sports, they love Cleveland's historically hapless (until recently) professional teams. And if they yearn for an outstanding quality of life, they love Cleveland's city center, the potential of its traditional neighborhoods, magnificent suburbs, and a scenic countryside only a short drive from downtown.

Cleveland A to Z is your short cut to understanding our great city, its salient attractions, history and mythologies. It's not a guidebook in the traditional sense, but a key to locating and unlocking the "Cleveland soul." It begins to answer the question of how anyone could love this place.

As a lifelong Clevelander, I am gratified by the range and depth of coverage in these pages. *Cleveland A to Z* includes Cleveland's general environs as well as its historic core. Here, you can learn about Cleveland's significant "firsts," like the original "Cleveland Indian," the world's first rock-and-roll concert, and the site of America's first red-yellow-green mechanical traffic signal.

You'll learn the history of Cleveland's legendary (if not totally explicable) East Side/West Side divide, the tales around the city's "most haunted house," and why the words Euclid Beach still summon the sounds of crashing waves and of a distant calliope for thousands of Cleveland old-timers.

Music lovers will head first for the history of Cleveland's renowned orchestra, and then to the entry on the Agora—a rock venue of national importance in the 1970s. They may also want to check out the story of Cleveland-style polka, a spry mix of Dixieland, sweet jazz, and Slovenian melodies that was born in our ethnic communities and may be the city's most distinctive folk creation.

In the 1920s, Cleveland was known as the Fifth City, coming right after Detroit on the list of America's largest cities. With its combination of leading-edge industries, innovation, and concentrated wealth, Cleveland was the Silicon Valley of the day. *Time* magazine moved its primary offices to Cleveland in the 1920s to partake of the city's progressive aura. At one time, Cleveland purportedly had more millionaires than any city in America, vying with Detroit to be the nation's number one manufacturer of automobiles.

From these pages sounds a roll of prominent names whose achievements still echo in the national consciousness: John D. Rockefeller, Louis Stokes, Carl Stokes, Jesse Owens, Eliot Ness, Marcus Hanna, "Chef Boyardee," and Alan Freed. There are also people whose names resonate strictly locally, but who are no less important to the city's history: people like Joc-O-Sot, Xenophon Zapis, and Short Vincent (not a man, but a street).

Few people know and love Cleveland like John Grabowski. He's an eminent historian and author of scholarly and popular books and articles about the city. But he's also a fan. His enthusiasm comes across in every entry of *Cleveland A to Z*. He appreciates Cleveland's eccentric splendor and honors its historic greatness. He has given us one of those rare reference books that can be read with equal pleasure from back to front, or dipped into at random, over your breakfast pierogi.

If *Cleveland A to Z* has whetted your appetite for Cleveland history and you find yourself hankering for more, I would strongly recommend a visit to the Cleveland History Center of the Western Reserve Historical Society (www.wrhs.org). This marvelous resource of displays, artifacts, and treasures of the city's history located in University Circle is your portal to the city and region's past. From the vintage carousel, to the Hanna and Hay-McKinney mansions, to the historic cars and planes, to the world-class costume collection and its nationally significant research library, its attractions are as many and varied as those of the region it represents.

"Into the flats, through Cleveland's / Steeple trees illuminated."

Allen Ginsberg, poet and noted member of the beat generation

THIS PUBLICATION IS MADE POSSIBLE BY THE GENEROUS SUPPORT OF

DON AND MARY JO DAILEY
ROBERT H. AND DONNA L. JACKSON

PREFACE

The first book on Cleveland history, the *Early History of Cleveland, Ohio, Including Original Papers and Other Matter Relating to the Adjacent Country*, was published by Fairbanks, Benedict and Co. in 1867. The history was written by Col. Charles Whittlesey, a founder of the Western Reserve Historical Society (WRHS) in 1867 and WRHS president from 1867 to 1887.

Over the last 150 years, as Whittlesey wished and expected, WRHS has been and remains the source for Cleveland and northeast Ohio history, ranking as one of the nation's largest and most diversified historical societies. To mark this milestone, WRHS is pleased to present *Cleveland A to Z* by Dr. John Grabowski, WRHS Chief Historian and Krieger-Mueller Associate Professor of Applied History at Case Western Reserve University. John brings his unparalleled knowledge of Cleveland history, expertise, and personal passion to this work, and for that WRHS is most grateful.

This book also continues in the traditions set by the institution's founders. Whittlesey and those who supported WRHS during its earliest and most vulnerable years were passionate not only about the collection and the preservation of original materials relating to local, regional, and national history, but also about the need to disseminate the knowledge embodied in those materials. For them, publications were the key to sharing this information.

The means of sharing knowledge based on the collections entrusted to this institution have expanded greatly since WRHS's founding. Exhibits, community events, school programming, hands-on experiences with our collections, and the vast potential of the internet now are among the many ways WRHS tells the story of Cleveland and northeast Ohio. The stories embodied in these collections are key to understanding who we are as a community and nation.

So what would Col. Whittlesey think if he visited us today? We know he would be proud—proud that the institution he helped found has endured and that it has grown and continues to prosper. We believe our founders would also be delighted that WRHS continues to publish. *Cleveland A to Z* is one of more than 200 books and tracts published by WRHS since 1870.

We are so pleased to continue this tradition with a guide to Cleveland for residents, newcomers, and visitors, touching upon topics ranging from mustard and pierogies to Whiskey Island and Vinegar Hill. Whether you are "from here," new to the area, or just visiting, *Cleveland A to Z* is your essential guide. Paired with Cleveland Starts Here®, WRHS's new permanent multimedia exhibit, rich with artifacts on the history of Cleveland and northeast Ohio, sponsored by the Jack, Joseph and Morton Mandel Foundation, this guide helps frame the important birthday that we as an institution celebrate this year.

Kelly Falcone-Hall
President and CEO, Western Reserve Historical Society

ACKNOWLEDGMENTS

Writing a book may seem a solitary project, but the reality of authorship is ultimately one of a partnership of support and assistance. *Cleveland A to Z* has been a long-term project, one that came to fruition because of institutional commitment and the support and encouragement of many friends and colleagues.

This volume began, so to speak, in 2011, when Dr. Gainor Davis, then President and CEO of the Western Reserve Historical Society, suggested that I write a book that would serve as a readable but solid historical introduction to Cleveland—a guidebook of sorts. She discerned a need for what might be considered a handbook for new arrivals to the city as well as for longtime residents who needed a quick refresher course on local history. She also felt it should be published by the Historical Society. This work thus owes its genesis to her; it represents her focus on the publishing tradition of the Society and its role as the center for Cleveland's history. As the Welsh would say, "diolch i chi" (thank you).

Kelly Falcone-Hall, President and CEO, has maintained and strongly supported the institution's traditional role as a publisher. It was her commitment to the project that has allowed it to come to publication. I was particularly delighted and honored when she suggested that the book be issued as part of the Historical Society's 150th anniversary program.

That landmark program has been made possible by the full team of WRHS staff and board members who have made this a very energetic, exciting, and satisfying sesquicentennial year. This book and the overall mission of the institution rest on their dedication, enthusiasm and support. Both now and in the past, a shared sense of history and understanding of its importance among all associated with WRHS have made it a very special place.

There are many others who have played a specific part in this project. The alphabetical arrangement of the topics echoes that of the *Encyclopedia of Cleveland History*, and I owe an enormous debt to the late Dr. David D. Van Tassel for asking me, many years ago, to join him in that pioneering project. More importantly, much of what I have come to know about the city derives from that project and from the hundreds of writers who contributed articles for the *Encyclopedia*. Their names are, as they say, far too many to list, but that does not diminish my gratitude for their contributions.

Robert Jackson, board member and chair of the Society's Publications Committee, has maintained a keen interest in the project as well as an unwavering commitment to the Society's publication program. He and his wife, Donna, provided support central to the completion of this book. Don Dailey, former board chair of WRHS, has never let the project off his radar screen. His enthusiasm and support—as well as the support from his wife, Mary Jo—have kept it, and me, moving forward.

Specific staff, past and present, at the Historical Society have been central to certain aspects of the project. As they say, "It takes a village." Ann Sindelar, Colleen Fedewa, Jane Mason, Angie Lowrie, and Alyssa Purvis, found images, scanned images, made constructive suggestions, and, in many ways, helped bring this manuscript together. Mary Thoburn and Lisa Leaman oversaw the budgeting and planning strategies that moved the project forward. Chad Malkamaki, Lead Interpreter at WRHS's Cleveland History Center, and John Baden, a graduate student at Case Western Reserve University and former associate editor of the online edition of the *Encyclopedia of Cleveland History*, used their technical prowess to create the QR codes in the text, and Chad has helped me keep a close eye on the facts.

I am particularly indebted to Lauren Pacini whose extraordinary contemporary images have brought this volume into the present and done so with style and imagination. One of my joys over the years has been to work with people with expertise and style—Lauren fits both categories perfectly. It is simply a delight to work and create with him. The same sentiments apply to Tim Lachina, whose design expertise has created a stunning whole from a number of pieces and parts.

Lastly, my thanks go to the many audiences in and around Cleveland who attended the lectures I have given on various aspects of the city's and the region's history. In many ways, my choice of articles for inclusion in the book is a compilation of their reactions to particular topics and certain historical trends and issues. I trust that this book reflects what they felt to be compelling and important, for the best thing a historian can do is to use the audience's interests to open an even wider window on the past.

John J. Grabowski

NOT YOUR TYPICAL CITY, NOT YOUR TYPICAL GUIDE

Cities around the globe, whether large or small, have characteristics that create a particular identity. Some loom large in our imagination—London is Big Ben, scarlet uniforms and pomp and ceremony; New York is bigness and bustle, the Statue of Liberty and canyons created by skyscrapers; and Istanbul, a swirl of minarets and the treasures of the Topkapi Palace. Even places not so fully within the popular imagination have their own auras. Massillon, Ohio, a mill city, is all about football; Newcastle-on-Tyne echoes of coal, ships, and Geordie culture; and Pushkar, India, is a camel fair wreathed in memories of the 1960s counterculture. None of these popular identities, of course, are entirely true, nor do they fully reflect the complexities of these communities. Nevertheless, they are the myths we want to believe.

What about Cleveland? What are its nuances, its images? Is Cleveland the Terminal Tower or is it the West Side Market? Or is it simply the city where LeBron James plays basketball? How do longtime residents view their community? Do they see only the past or do they look to the future? What do newcomers need to know about their new hometown? How can you pronounce Cuyahoga so as not to seem a newbie? Does it really matter if you cannot explain why the city has a Public Square? Most importantly, how can one "find" Cleveland within the urban legends, slogans, and marketing imagery that continually adjust to a particular time or need?

Images and image makers aside, what makes Cleveland problematic, particularly for new residents, is the fact that non-Clevelanders know so little about it. And what they do know is sometimes unflattering or totally off the historical mark. The city is sometimes difficult to explain. Where is it? My usual answer is "in northeast Ohio." But that has little meaning for someone outside of the United States. So the next locater is to say "on Lake Erie between New York and Chicago." That helps, but it also places the city in a shadow in which it has always existed, both in the popular conception and also in historical studies. It creates a diminution of sorts—it becomes a place known only because of its relationship to far better-known places. But that is unfair. Cleveland is not Chicago and it is not New York. Its landmarks, local quirks, historical persona, and unique landscape make it what it is: a city that is global and parochial at the same time, a community that played a significant role in the growth of the nation, but often ends up as an also-ran in the historical sweepstakes, and a community whose reality is far deeper than the clichéd images and stories that have served as popular descriptors.

This volume is a guide, not to the usual topics—landmarks, restaurants, shopping, and notable this's and that's—but to places, people, stories, and events, which also hint at the deeper themes that define Cleveland. It is a history of sorts, certainly not deep or comprehensive, but a light and sometimes tongue-in-cheek chronicle that should prove immediately helpful to newcomers and, I hope, instructive to long-time residents. Its structure is alphabetical—a scheme shamelessly cribbed from the *Encyclopedia of Cleveland History*. The selection of its content, while very personal—and seemingly arbitrary at first glance—rested upon a particular topic's relevance to those themes that make the city what it is—cosmopolitan, sometimes divisive, accomplished, and sometimes overly consumed by and concerned about its past.

It is also a guide to the various pathways that will allow readers to explore the community in more detail. Some of the entries are accompanied by citations and most by QR codes that lead to other sources of information. Cleveland is particularly lucky to have had so many people who were fascinated by its story and, in their own manner, felt compelled to write scores of books about the community and, more recently, to create blogs, websites, and apps that help illuminate the past and the issues facing the community today. Three of these sources, the *Encyclopedia of Cleveland History* (ech.cwru.edu), a project of Case Western Reserve University and the Western Reserve Historical Society; the Cleveland Memory Project website (www.clevelandmemory.org) at Cleveland State University; and the Cleveland Historical app and site (clevelandhistorical.org), also at CSU, provide links for almost every article in this guide.

If you want to know Cleveland, start here. But don't stop here; pursue the city's past on its streets, in its museums and libraries, and in the conversations you have with other Clevelanders. Then decide on your own as to what the essence of this city is.

AGORA

Scan to learn more

While the Moondog Coronation Ball marks the beginning of Cleveland's link to the history of rock and roll, the Cleveland Agora is the ongoing connection to the city's role in rock history during what was arguably one of the genre's greatest eras—the 1970s and 1980s.

The Agora began in 1967 as a dance club for college students. It was located at Cornell and Random Roads, just off the Case Western Reserve campus in a building now occupied by Club Isabella. Admitting members only at first, the Agora featured local bands. A year later it moved downtown to East 24th Street near Cleveland State University. In 1987 it moved to its current location in the old Metropolitan Theater on Euclid Avenue just west of East 55th Street.

What was critical about the Agora was not so much where it was located, but what went on within those locations. Founder, Henry J. "Hank" LoConti (1929–2014) featured local bands and talent from the very beginning. By the 1970s, he was taking chances on new bands and singers touring the nation who were offering new forms of the rock genre. During the 1970s, the Agora would host Bruce Springsteen, Southside Johnny, Kiss, the local Michael Stanley Band, and other groups at the cutting-edge of music. The live sounds at the Agora were paralleled by the music programmed by local FM station WMMS during the 1970s and 1980s.

"The Buzzard," both the nickname and the logo for the station, symbolized new music, such as punk and heavy metal, that challenged tradition. Together, 'MMS and the Agora represented what young people wanted. It can be argued that the Agora helped set those styles on firm footing. Hank LoConti would open over a dozen branches of the nightclub in Ohio and around the nation during the venue's heyday.

The Agora rocks on today. Its rich history is a part of the personal memory of many who attended its concerts. And, thanks to the foresight of Hank LoConti, those concerts live on in the incredible Agora Archive preserved at the Western Reserve Historical Society.

Henry J. ("Hank") LoConti, one of the pivotal figures in Cleveland's "Rock" history.

The entrance to the Agora Theatre.

MOSES ALSBACHER (1805–1874)

Scan to learn more

A portrait (ca. 1860) of Moses Alsbacher and the document he carried from Bavaria to Cleveland in 1839.

Moses Alsbacher was one of the tens of thousands of immigrants who have chosen to come to northeastern Ohio over the past two centuries. While his story is similar to those of other immigrants, both past and present, it is, in some ways, quite special.

Alsbacher was the leader of a group of nineteen Jews who emigrated from Unsleben, Bavaria, in 1839. It was a time when many people, both Jews and Christians, were leaving for America from the various states and principalities that now constitute Germany. Cleveland and northeastern Ohio would receive a huge number of German-speaking immigrants during the nineteenth century, and, indeed, German was, by the post–Civil War era, the second language of Cleveland. However, the arrival of the Alsbacher party in Cleveland was special, as it marked the beginning of a permanent Jewish community in northeastern Ohio. A few Jewish settlers had come to the region earlier but there was no cohesive community until one of the early visitors, Simson Thorman, saw potential in the growing canal-era city of Cleveland and invited the group from Unsleben (his hometown) to join him. He met the group of immigrants in New York and convinced all but two to follow him to what was then a town of about 6,000.

The "Alsbacher Party" brought with them all that was needed to start a Jewish community: enough male adults to form a minyan to allow for public worship, a shochet who could perform ritual slaughter according to the laws of kashrut, and a mohel able to perform circumcision. But they also brought something else—a set of instructions from their rabbi, Lazarus Kohn, in Unsleben. It lists all the members of the Alsbacher party and the names of those Jews who remained in Unsleben. Most importantly, in the form of an ethical testament, it asks that those who left to continue to honor and hold fast to the religion of their forefathers in a land of new and tempting freedoms.

This document, written for a group of Jewish immigrants, is remarkable in many ways. It has survived through the decades and is now preserved in the research library of the Western Reserve Historical Society. However, it is more than a foundational document for the Jewish community. Lazarus Kohn's words about holding true to one's tradition and culture in a land of tempting freedoms transcend religion, nationality, and ethnicity. They define the challenge that nearly every immigrant faces in a new homeland—what to keep and what to change, how to fit in and how to find continuity. In a city and region that is now home to over 100 different ethnic groups, the little handwritten booklet carried across the sea from Unsleben has a more universal and deeper resonance today than ever before.

Rubinstein, Judah, and Jane Avner. *Merging Traditions: Jewish Life in Cleveland.* Kent, OH: Kent State Univ. Press, 2004.

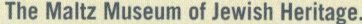
The Maltz Museum of Jewish Heritage.

ANDREWS'S FOLLY

Scan to learn more

What happens when an English immigrant to Cleveland decides to build a house large and lavish enough to entertain Queen Victoria? Answer: the Queen doesn't turn up and not only is the owner left with a home that is too difficult to operate, but the layout and maintenance are a burden on the family and staff. However, more importantly, Cleveland gains a legendary structure that epitomizes the lifestyle and sometimes oversize dreams of the residents of "Millionaires' Row," which stretched along a good portion of Euclid Avenue.

Samuel Andrews was a candle maker who came to Cleveland in 1857. He used his basic skills to learn how to refine kerosene from crude oil, a talent that would become immensely valuable when Cleveland became a refining center after the Pennsylvania oil boom of the late 1850s, and particularly when he went into partnership with John D. Rockefeller in 1863. He was one of the founding partners of Standard Oil in 1870. In 1874 he and Rockefeller were not seeing eye to eye, so he cashed out of the company for $1 million, a huge sum at the time, but not much compared to what he would have accumulated had he stayed with Standard.

Bleak, dirty, and isolated, a view of the Andrews mansion shortly before it was demolished in the 1920s.

He built his dream house on the northeast corner of Euclid and East 30th Street between 1882 and 1885. It had an estimated 80 to 100 rooms, including a complete apartment suite for each of his six children (accounts of the interior arrangements tend to differ). After living in the massive home for three years, he moved to New York and, with the exception of short stays by his son Horace, the house sat empty until 1923 when it was razed. Perhaps its last claim to fame was the commercial miniature golf course that graced its expansive front lawn in the years just after World War I.

Most of the grand homes on Euclid were demolished. Many, like the Andrews house, represented the dreams of the newly rich in the Gilded Age, who eagerly put their success on display. Yet, Millionaires' Row remains a significant Cleveland memory—a talisman of an imagined grand past that often ignores less grandiose aspects of the Gilded Age. Today the best way to experience Euclid Avenue is to ride the Health Line with a copy of Jan Cigliano's excellent book, *Showplace of America*, in hand.

A handful of houses, some grand, some not so grand, and some hidden behind new facades, can still be found if you look carefully.

Cigliano, Jan. *Showplace of America*. Kent, OH: Kent State Univ. Press, 1991.

Street scene across what was once the Andrews estate.

BIRDTOWN (aka Bird's Nest)

Scan to learn more

Churches representing the immigrants who settled in Birdtown.

Thrush, Plover, Quail, Robin, and Lark—these are street names in a Lakewood neighborhood known as Birdtown (or the Bird's Nest) that seem to hint at a birder's paradise or, at the very least, a rich ornithological history. Instead, they have more to do with technology, industry, and immigration at the turn of the twentieth century.

The National Carbon Company created the neighborhood in the 1890s to house workers at its plant on West 117th Street. That plant was dealing with cutting-edge technology at the time—including the production of dry cell batteries, an important component of the electrical revolution occurring in the United States and around the world at that time. And, as in many cases with industrial expansion in Cleveland at the time, the world came to the city looking for work. Many of those who came to work at National Carbon were Slovaks from the Austro-Hungarian Empire. They constituted almost 70 percent of the neighborhood's population. Others included Poles and Ukrainians. As the population grew, the immigrants found jobs at other industries, including the Winton Motor Company and Glidden Paints, both located along the nearby rail line.

The role of heavy industry in this borderland between Cleveland and Lakewood is memorialized by repurposed factory buildings and by Carbon Street, which runs between West 117th and Berea Road, but more so by the neighborhood it created, where churches such as St. Cyril and Methodius (now merged into Transfiguration Parish) reflect on a global past, and former "mom and pop" stores host new ventures, making Birdtown a revitalized urban scene on the eastern edge of Lakewood.

Pankuch, Jan. *History of the Slovaks of Cleveland and Lakewood*. Translated by Rasto Gallo. Cleveland: Western Reserve Historical Society, 2001.

Slovaks were one of the immigrant groups that worked in the industries in the Bird's Nest area of Lakewood. This "Slovak Family" group was part of a 1939 civic parade.

HECTOR (ETTORE) BOIARDI (1897–1985)

Scan to learn more

Cleveland's restaurant scene is considered one of the best in the nation today, a reputation built, in part, on the many ethnic cuisines offered throughout the city and region. Given this, it should be no surprise that the man who helped popularize Italian foods to the general public began that mass-market enterprise in Cleveland.

Born in Italy, Boiardi was a classically trained Italian chef who came to New York circa 1914 and first worked in the Ritz Carlton. He moved to Cleveland in 1917, cooking at the prestigious Hotel Winton where his spaghetti dishes garnered rave reviews. Seven years later he opened his own restaurant, the Giardino d'Italia at East 9th and Woodland, then the very northern tip of what was known as the Big Italy neighborhood. It was both a dine-in and carry-out operation and soon was hugely successful. Success continued into and during the Great Depression because Boiardi had chosen to focus on affordable, mass-produced foods that, while Italian in origin, were aimed at the general American market. In 1938 the company moved to Milton, Pennsylvania, to be closer to farms that could produce the vast numbers of tomatoes needed for his then mass-marketed canned meals. Boiardi sold the company for nearly $6 million shortly after World War II, but he remained a consultant and its on-camera TV spokesperson until 1978.

Today you most likely will not find Spaghetti Rings or Beefaroni in any of Cleveland's many Italian restaurants, but you will find people of a variety of backgrounds enjoying Italian cuisines, ranging from Tuscan to Sicilian. The fact that they are there can, in part, be attributed to the role Ettore Boiardi played in familiarizing the public with Italian food. He did so knowing that Italian culture was terra incognita for many—something best evidenced by his last name.

Interior of the former Saint Anthony's Catholic Church, which served the lower Woodland Avenue Italian neighborhood known as Big Italy.

Knowing most Americans could not pronounce Boiardi, he transliterated it to Boyardee—and, to make matters even clearer, he broke it down into syllables—BOY-AR-DEE—on the chef's toque he wore during his many television commercials.

The dining room of the Hotel Winton, ca. 1910, where Hector Boiardi served as chef.

CLEVELAND A to Z

THE BRIDGE WAR

Scan to learn more

For a community noted for the number and variety of its bridges, it is somewhat ironic that some citizens were so upset with the first permanent structure across the Cuyahoga River that they tried to destroy it.

The dissatisfaction was not about the aesthetics of the bridge, but rather about its potential economic impact. Opened in April 1836 on Columbus Street, the bridge provided a direct and easy route to Cleveland markets and businesses for farmers living west of the river. That meant, however, that they might discontinue their regular path to the markets and businesses in Ohio City, the separate community that existed on the west bank of the Cuyahoga. What ensued was a failed attempt to destroy the bridge, an attempt in which a group of Cleveland militiamen fought off the would-be saboteurs from Ohio City.

Today this incident is viewed as a slightly humorous piece of early local lore—despite the fact that three people were seriously wounded and a number arrested. Moreover, it represents something of real consequence about the city. Cleveland on the east bank and Ohio City on the west bank were legally separate and intense economic rivals. Indeed, the fact that Ohio City had achieved official status as a city on March 3, 1836, and Cleveland two days later was a matter not taken lightly by Clevelanders. Eventually, in 1854, Ohio City merged into Cleveland, which, by that time, had become the larger and economically stronger of the two.

Today, a vertical lift bridge stands at the site of the first bridge. Visit it, walk the area, and look carefully at the immense breadth of the Flats (see The Flats). This makes it much easier to appreciate the vast physical separation between the two communities—a separation that makes "East Sider or West Sider" a common part of any contemporary introductory conversation.

The Columbus Street Bridge as depicted on a mid-1830s map of Cleveland prepared by Ahaz Merchant.

This image shows the fifth span of the Columbus Street Bridge. It was installed and opened in 2014.

CLEVELAND A to Z

BURNING RIVER

Scan to learn more

The term "Burning River" has become something of a symbol of Clevelanders' ability to deal with adversity. Used to describe everything from a locally brewed pale ale to the city's roller derby team, it derives from one of the most nationally embarrassing moments in the city's history—the day the Cuyahoga River burned. But that event in 1969, like many instances in the community's history, is surrounded by mythology.

The river did not burn on June 22, 1969. Rather an accumulation of flammable waste below a wooden railroad trestle caught fire. This wasn't the first time debris on the river caught fire, nor was it the most spectacular conflagration on the water. In 1952 an oil slick on the river caught fire causing $1.5 million in damage, particularly to the facilities of the Great Lakes Towing Company. Unlike the 1969 fire, this one got very little national notice. At that time, the use of urban rivers as routes for industrial effluent was a tolerated practice in the United States. But in 1969, the nation had become well aware of the environmental degradation created by the misuse of natural resources. The anomaly of a flaming waterway was truly shocking—so much so that historians believe that the Burning River in Cleveland was a factor in the creation of the EPA in 1970.

The effectiveness of that legislation can be seen on and in the Cuyahoga River today. While still hosting industries and ore freighters, it is now again home to fish as well as to crew races and urban boating. It is not yet the perfect waterway, but it stands as the phoenix still rising from its own flames and a symbol of both the past and future of the city.

Should you wish to visit the sites of the two fires, take one of the scheduled river tours that leave from the East Ninth Street Pier and be certain to have a bottle of Burning River before you embark.

By the 1880s, when this photo was taken, the Cuyahoga River was crowded and already heavily polluted.

A tribute to the river's legacy, installed on the Mall in 2013.

CEDAR AVENUE

Scan to learn more

Shauter Drug at 9208 Cedar was one of a number of African American owned enterprises along the avenue in its heyday.

The home of Antioch Baptist Church since 1924.

Once upon a time Cedar Avenue was Cleveland's answer to East 125th Street in New York's Harlem. From the 1920s into the 1960s, it, along with parallel Central Avenue, formed the east-west spine of Cleveland's African American community. Stretching from downtown to University Circle, Cedar-Central was home to nearly 95 percent of the city's African American population during the 1930s, a time when de facto segregation was the norm in the city. Like Harlem, it was a place where African Americans "had" to reside, but one they made into a vibrant, entrepreneurial neighborhood. Black-owned businesses—including funeral homes, such as Boyd; restaurants, like Art's Seafood; and a number of churches, such as St. James AME and Antioch Baptist—lined Cedar Avenue. The Cedar Gardens and Val's In the Alley were entertainment venues, which, like New York City's Apollo, attracted both black and white audiences. A young Jesse Owens worked as a service station attendant at Alonzo Wright's Sohio Station at East 93rd and Cedar. Owens would become an Olympian hero, and Wright would rise to become Cleveland's first black millionaire whose effort to move out to a suburb was met with a bomb thrown through the window of his home in the 1930s. Allen E. Cole, whose studio was at 9904 Cedar, photographed Wright and Owens and many of the businesses, churches, and clubs along the street.

Today a drive along Cedar Avenue provides some glimpses into what once was. It is still lined with churches, and Boyd Funeral Home still operates at East 89th. But much of the old Cedar-Central neighborhood (now part of the Cedar and Fairfax planning districts) lives on only in the memories of former residents and in the photographs of Allen E. Cole, whose archives are one of the treasures of the Western Reserve Historical Society.

Black, Samuel, and Regennia Williams. *Through the Lens of Allen E. Cole: A Photographic History of African Americans in Cleveland, Ohio.* Kent, OH: Kent State Univ. Press in Cooperation with the Western Reserve Historical Society, 2012.

CLEVELAND A to Z

CHRISTMAS STORIES

Scan to learn more

When a Clevelander begins talking about a Christmas story, don't immediately assume that it's personal. It is most likely about the 1983 movie, *A Christmas Story*, which is a local obsession, given that parts of it were filmed in Cleveland. One of the sets, a house on West 11th Street in the Tremont neighborhood, is now a museum honoring the film. You can immediately recognize it by the leg lamp in the front window. Part of the lure of the movie for Clevelanders is the role played by the former Higbee's Department Store on Public Square. It was the site of many holiday shopping ventures for the boomer generation.

Today, its art moderne building houses the JACK Casino. But the fictional story of Ralphie, BB guns, and a tongue frozen to a flagpole is trumped by a true Cleveland Christmas story.

On December 24, 1851, Rev. Heinrich Schwan introduced a new holiday tradition to Cleveland. The recently appointed pastor of Zion Evangelical Lutheran Church brought a candle-lit Christmas tree into the sanctuary of the church, thus transplanting an old Germanic tradition to Cleveland. It was one of the first Christmas trees in the nation. The auspicious event did not go unnoticed. Conservative local Protestants called it a "heathenish custom, this groveling before the shrubs." Nearly a century later, in 1935, the May Company, Higbee's competitor on Public Square, placed a large tree on Public Square, starting a tradition that endures to today and also making a statement of sorts on the site that was the New England town commons for early Cleveland.

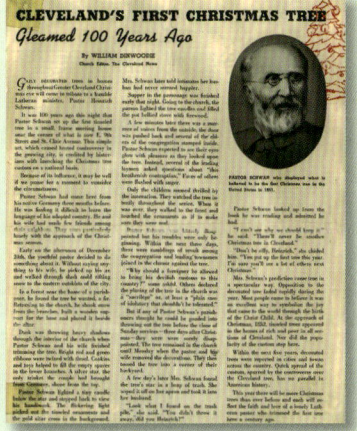

Rev. Heinrich Schwan shocked the community when he carried on a long-standing German tradition and placed a Christmas tree in Zion Evangelical Lutheran Church.

The "Christmas Story House," transformed into the Parkers' house.

CLEVELAND A to Z

MOSES CLEAVELAND (1754–1806)

Scan to learn more

Rolf Stoll's 1952 painting of Moses Cleaveland has become the quintessential image of the city's founder.

Revolutionary War soldier, Yale graduate, legislator, lawyer, and real estate speculator—these terms are certainly descriptive of the founder of Cleveland, Ohio, even though the last descriptor might seem jarring and a bit irreverent. But, Cleaveland was a man of his times and like many leading figures in colonial America he was entrepreneurial and knew the importance of land both as investment and necessity in a largely rural nation.

That interest led him to become one of the investors in and a director of the Connecticut Land Company, which purchased Connecticut's Western Reserve from that state in 1795, the same year that Native American rights to the lands east of the Cuyahoga River were "extinguished" by the Treaty of Greenville. Cleaveland had leadership skills that prompted his corporate peers to select him for the task of leading a survey party to the Reserve in order to assess and divide the lands for sale.

He arrived at the Cuyahoga River on July 22, 1796. His initial thought was to name the city after the river, but members of the party suggested that it carry his name. With that settled, he and the surveyors began the laborious process of bringing logic to the landscape, dividing the land into five-mile-square townships and envisioning the region as similar to New England. The town square they laid out (today's Public Square) is a lasting reminder of their cultural vision.

Cleaveland returned home in October and never again visited the settlement that bore his name. His report to his fellow directors was, in part, visionary. He felt that Cleveland would one day be as large as Windham, Connecticut, then a town of 2,700 people. It would take more than three decades for that to occur.

What he did not predict was how he might be remembered. He may or may not have expressed dismay at the manipulation of his surname: Cleaveland became Cleveland. While stories abound as to why this occurred, records indicate that both spellings were used concurrently. Indeed, some early documents relating to the community do not use the initial "a" in its name. In 1831 the *Cleveland Advertiser* newspaper formally dropped the "a" from its masthead and informed its readers that it was superfluous. That aside, Cleaveland might be honored by the statue erected to him on the city's Public Square in 1888. But here again the community tampered with his legacy. Some felt the first plaster model of the statue made him too tall—it was remedied by removing a section of his midsection. And, when members of the city's chamber of commerce restored his overgrown gravesite in Canterbury, Connecticut, in 1906, they erected a memorial describing him as "a lawyer, a soldier, a legislator, and a leader of men." It was a fitting tribute, but it seems somewhat ironic that men of commerce would forget that he was also an entrepreneurial risk taker.

The city's founder, given by the Early Settlers Association in 1888.

CLEVELAND CULTURAL GARDENS

Scan to learn more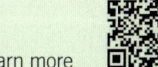

Members of various Italian American organizations pose at the dedication of the Italian Cultural Garden in 1930.

Residents of northeastern Ohio take enormous pride in their ethnic roots. One of the usual questions upon meeting someone new to the area is "what are you?" That can be confusing to someone not familiar with the ways of the city. Certainly the responses can cover a gamut of personal identities and occupations. But the question is all about ethnicity and nationality. That "what are you" aspect of the community is on permanent memorial display in the Cleveland Cultural Gardens, a series of landscaped areas with statues and plaques that honor the culture and cultural heroes of various immigrant and ethnic communities in northeastern Ohio. The gardens stretch along the east and west sides of Martin Luther King Jr. Boulevard in Rockefeller Park. This manifestation of regional cultural memory began in 1916 with the establishment of the Shakespeare Garden (today known as the British Garden); since then another twenty-six gardens were established and, as of this writing, more are on the way.

While the gardens honor individual ethnic groups, their history says much about Cleveland and the sometimes contentious issue of diversity in America. The fact that the gardens really began to grow in the 1920s is startling in historical perspective. This was the decade in which immigration to the United States was severely restricted. It was an era of 100 percent Americanism in the United States—yet Cleveland insisted on celebrating the diversity and cultures of its many communities. But there were problems in honoring that diversity. Community committees that oversaw the establishment of a particular garden debated and contended as to which cultural heroes would be included. The focus of the gardens was on the great and famous from a particular group, not on the ordinary immigrant who had come to work in the city's industries. The statue of an immigrant mother in the recent (2009) Croatian Garden highlights a change from that viewpoint. The new Croatian garden reflects another aspect of diversity and change— the community was once part of the Yugoslav Garden, which today is the Slovenian Garden. The Serbs, once part of that garden and the post–World War I nation of the South Slavs now also have their own along the boulevard. Then there was the issue of race.

The white ethnic communities that surrounded the gardens were replaced by African American neigh-borhoods in the 1950s and 1960s, yet the gardens at that time honored only one African American, Booker T. Washington, and his bust was in the American Garden.

Within the past twenty years, the gardens have grown enormously and have embraced a newer view of diversity, one that reflects the changes in immigration and migration to Cleveland since the 1960s. With more than 100 ethnicities resident in the region, there is a huge potential for expansion in the gardens. An African American Garden has been established as well as Chinese, Azeri, and Asian Indian gardens. The latter garden features a larger-than-life statue of Gandhi. The fact that Gandhi stands along what is now Martin Luther King Jr. Boulevard reminds passersby that the core theme of the gardens is Peace—and, indeed, the gardens have served to open an ongoing community discussion on that topic.

One World Day dedication of the Albanian and Croatian gardens in 2012.

THE CLEVELAND ORCHESTRA

Scan to learn more

Characterized as the "best band in the land," the Cleveland Orchestra really needs no introduction to newcomers or longtime citizens of Cleveland—it is a part of the community's cultural infrastructure known from Tokyo to Salzburg. But, like everything in Cleveland, there are parts of the story that remain largely unknown.

Adella Prentiss Hughes (1869–1950), the woman who built the foundation for the Cleveland Orchestra.

In the case of the orchestra, it is the fact that its creation was engineered by a woman who loved music, and her story opens up the broader story of women in Cleveland in the nineteenth century.

Adella Prentiss Hughes (1869–1950) was a local musical impresario. Born in Cleveland, she graduated from Vassar in 1890 with a degree in music. Her post-graduation grand tour of Europe brought her into contact with some of the major figures in nineteenth-century classical music. When she came back to Cleveland she undertook the task of bringing fine music to the city. Clevelanders wanted good music and, indeed, some were jealous that their Ohio urban rival, Cincinnati, had already established its own symphony orchestra by the 1890s. After nearly two decades of securing some of the finest musical talent for concerts in Cleveland, Hughes created the Musical Arts Association in 1915. Supported by leading businessmen, the association, Hughes, and conductor Nikolai Sokoloff came together in 1918 to create the orchestra. It may have been their money and Sokoloff's talent, but it was Hughes's vision and persistence that created the foundation for the best band in the land. That she did so is not surprising when you consider her heritage. Her maternal grandmother, Rebecca Rouse, was a vibrant leader in Cleveland in the years before, during, and after the Civil War. She was a founder of First Baptist Church, the organizer of the Soldiers' Aid Society, and one of the founders of what is now Beechbrook, formerly the Cleveland Protestant Orphan Asylum. A bas-relief plaque honors her Civil War work in the Soldiers and Sailors Monument on Public Square.

The story of women, culture, and art in Cleveland certainly does not begin or end with Adella Prentiss Hughes. The founder of the city's Music Settlement was Almeda Adams, and the hall in which the Cleveland Orchestra plays was funded by John Long Severance and named in honor of his late wife, Elisabeth. She, like almost all of the members of the family, was a believer in and supporter of the arts.

Perhaps a concert at Severance Hall is a good place to begin contemplating the still largely untold story of women in northeastern Ohio. An after-concert walk down East Boulevard will bring one to a monument and statue honoring the late Stephanie Tubbs Jones, congresswoman from Cleveland. Going in the opposite direction and into the campus of Case Western Reserve will bring you to the Bolton School of Nursing, named in honor of congresswoman Frances Bolton. Then there is the quadrangle

One of 14 murals by Else Vick Shaw in the Severance Hall's Grand Foyer.

of what was the Flora Stone Mather College for Women, which has two buildings named in her honor. Journeying farther afield down Martin Luther King Jr. Boulevard takes you to a statue of an anonymous but universal immigrant woman in the Croatian Cultural Garden. This journey brings together bits and pieces of a larger story central to Cleveland's As to Zs.

Morton, Marian J. *Women in Cleveland: An Illustrated History.* Bloomington: Indiana Univ. Press, 1995.

CUYAHOGA RIVER

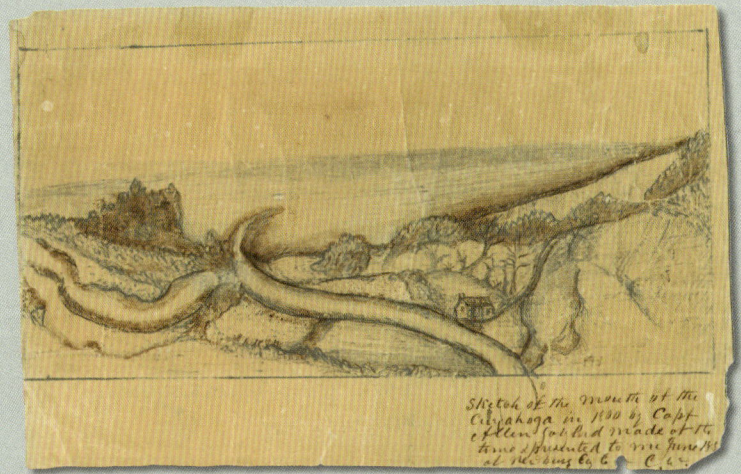

Sketched from memory in 1860 by Capt. Allen Gaylord, this drawing shows the mouth of the Cuyahoga River as it looked ca. 1800.

Simply stated, Cleveland would not exist if it were not for the Cuyahoga River. Benjamin Franklin envisioned its mouth on Lake Erie as strategic, and George Washington saw the river as a component of a potential waterway linking Lake Erie with the Ohio River. It was a logical site for the capital of the Western Reserve.

They weren't the first to take notice of the waterway. Native Americans used it for travel, fished its waters for food, and named it. In the Iroquoian language Cuyahoga means "crooked river," certainly an apt description—not only for the winding section in Cleveland's Flats but for the entirety of the waterway; it starts in Hamden in Geauga County and then flows south to Cuyahoga Falls where it turns north and wiggles its way to Lake Erie. While providing a name, the area's true first residents neglected to provide a pronunciation guide. So the newcomer to the city wonders if it should be Cuyahoga with a long o or with a short o. It's one of those Fred Astaire moments—potato, potahto, tomato, tomahto. One could call the whole thing off by noting that the *Webster's New World Dictionary* gives three variants for pronouncing the "o" in the third syllable as well as variants for the first syllable. But that's not going to help if you have a conversation with a native Clevelander who is on the short o side of the story or the long o side. The best choice (albeit, not terribly valorous) is to ask and then, once having learned the right way to pronounce the name, be prepared to be corrected in a future conversation.

The name aside, the waterway did prove to be one of the central factors in the city's growth and in its sometimes schizophrenic persona. Washington's vision of a waterway came to fruition in 1832 when the Ohio and Erie Canal linked Cleveland with Portsmouth on the Ohio River. It and its broad valley, the Flats, are the keys to the community's compulsive focus on East Side versus West Side. And the use and misuse of its waters for more than two centuries of settlement have been responsible for the city's industrial fortunes and its most notable national environmental misfortune—the Cuyahoga River fire of 1969 (see Burning River).

A lake freighter winds its way to the steel mills.

DOAN BROOK

Scan to learn more

Doan Brook is, in many ways, as influential a waterway for Cleveland as is the Cuyahoga River. While the former can be closely associated with the city's economic development, the latter has much to do with the culture, parks, and recreational development that came in the wake of economic prosperity. It was the defining locational factor for University Circle and its path the spine for a series of parks that begins at its mouth on Lake Erie and extends into Shaker Heights.

It is named after Nathanial Doan, an early settler who established a hotel, tavern, and blacksmith shop in 1799 at what is now Stokes Boulevard and Euclid. The stream, which crossed Euclid just east of Doan's establishment, was a natural stopping point on the road. Doan prospered as did farmers, such as the Fords and Cozads who

Dams, culverts, and channels, resulting in challenges of water quality and control.

As late as the 1890s, when this image was taken near St. Clair Avenue, the Doan Brook Valley remained undeveloped and quite pastoral.

lived in the area, which was a thriving satellite community by the time of the Civil War.

Change came when wealthy Clevelanders found the pastoral brook area an ideal rural getaway. William Gordon built his private park at the mouth of the stream, while Jeptha Wade bought the area north of Euclid. Both of their private parks would eventually be given to the city and later, in 1896, joined by Rockefeller Park to create a contiguous greenbelt, connecting University Circle, an evolving cultural center, to the lake.

This process of change also altered the brook—portions were channeled or completely culverted. It is, most ironically, invisible at Euclid Avenue, the point where its presence attracted the settlement of its namesake.

DOWNTOWN

Scan to learn more

As is the case in many older cities, Cleveland's downtown is encumbered with memories, most of which relate to the decades immediately after the Second World War, a time when industrial cities like Cleveland hit a brilliant peak before they began to wane.

Downtown was Cleveland for the first seven decades of its history, an era when the city's population was relatively small and walking was the most common mode of urban travel. The downtown included business, industry, and residential districts. By the 1890s, however, the center of the city was given over to offices, industry, and retail commerce—in which the department store became the epitome of big-city life and style. So it was in Cleveland, and in the postwar period the department stores were at their urban apogee. That's where the memories linger in the city—dressed up excursions, particularly during the holiday season to shop or just window shop along Euclid Avenue and, perhaps, Prospect. Stores like Halles, Sterling Lindner, and, to a large degree, Higbee's attracted an upscale clientele. Taylors and the May Company held a firm middle ground. With the mass movement to the suburbs in the 1950s, some of the stores built branches in malls such as Southgate. Halle's was one of the first to branch into the suburbs, including a store at Shaker Square in 1948.

By the 1980s, as was the case elsewhere in urban America, the big downtown stores were being bought out by chains (if, indeed, they were not already part of one) or closed while their suburban branches tended to prosper. Those branches with vast parking lots and absent the walk-by clientele did not have the rich window displays of their parent stores. Memories of those displays as well as escalator rides through the multiple floors of goods (with toys at the top at the old May Company) began to grow and today remain part of local boomer nostalgia.

Today there is only one old downtown store you can visit, but it can be risky business. The old Higbee's store next to the Terminal Tower is now the JACK Casino. If Santa happens to be there when you visit, ask him for the odds at roulette.

Karberg, Richard, and James Toman. *Euclid Avenue: Cleveland's Sophisticated Lady, 1920–1970*. Cleveland: Cleveland Landmarks Press, 2002.

A view of downtown from the roof of The 9.

A postcard view shows the heart of downtown Cleveland ca. 1910, when the city was the sixth-largest in the nation.

CLEVELAND A to Z

EMERALD NECKLACE

Scan to learn more

Henry Church, a local blacksmith and artist, carved this mystical figure of an Indian woman in 1885 beside the Chagrin River in what is now the South Chagrin Reservation of the Metroparks.

It is, in historical perspective, somewhat ironic that Greater Cleveland boasts one of the finest park systems of any urban area in the United States. During the nineteenth century, the city seemed to pay little attention to creating new green spaces, perhaps because the central Public Square was the accepted open commons for the community. Only in the 1870s did the city create other small open areas, several of which, such as Miles Park (originally the town common of Newburgh) and Franklin Circle, still survive. Fifty years later, however, the situation had changed drastically.

Gifts of private land from Jeptha Homer Wade and William J. Gordon anchored the south and north ends of a parkway that developed on the East Side. There was some dispute about accepting the Wade gift (1882) as the city felt it too distant from the center and had concerns about the cost of its upkeep. Linked by Rockefeller Park, a centennial gift to the city by John D. Rockefeller in 1896, they came to form a linked parkway from University Circle to the lake. On the West Side, the city purchased Joseph Perkins's beachfront property and in 1894 created what is now Edgewater Park.

By the turn of the century, the city had 1,200 acres of parkland within its boundaries—a 120 percent increase over the ten-acre Public Square, which constituted its only green space some forty years earlier. The new open spaces were welcome additions of green for a growing city that had become increasingly crowded and polluted by its industries.

Yet the best was to come. In the early 1900s, William Stinchcomb, a surveyor and later a city engineer, planned a grand set of parks surrounding the expanding urban area. Showing a persistence and vision typical of the leadership of the city in the Progressive era, Stinchcomb secured the legislation necessary to create what is now the Cleveland Metroparks and began the process of acquiring properties in Cuyahoga and Medina Counties. The process was not easy and it was not without controversy as private lands were incorporated into a continuous band of parks and parkways that stretched from the Rocky River valley on the west, to the south, and then up the Chagrin River valley on the east. During the Great Depression, WPA funds and laborers helped improve the parkway, which became known as the Emerald Necklace.

Today the system of parks is a pride of the area and one of the selling points for attracting new residents to the area. Where else can a community promise every citizen and new arrival an "Emerald Necklace"?

The 10th fairway of Acacia Country Club returning to nature.

CLEVELAND A to Z

ERIE

Scan to learn more

There are a number of "Erie" things and locations in and around Cleveland, including a hockey team (prior to mid-2016), a cemetery, and a lake. Then there are things in the city's past that were once Erie, such as the street (now East 9th), after which the cemetery is named, and the allegorical marine monster—described in the city's first newspaper, the *Cleveland Gazette and Commercial Register* in 1818—which is the ancestor of the current hockey team's former name.

Indeed, the name Erie opens up all sorts of possibilities for historical discussion. Take the cemetery and the street, for example. Erie Street was the original eastern boundary of the community and the cemetery, which opened in 1826 and was placed just outside the perimeter of the community. This says something about initial expectations for the size of the community. As the city expanded, the land became more valuable for the living than the dead. That it mostly survived, rather than being turned to a more useful purpose, is testament to early preservation efforts in Cleveland.

As for hockey teams, the Lake Erie Monsters (as of 2016 the Cleveland Monsters) are the most recent in a series of teams, including the Indians, Falcons, Barons (the best remembered of all the franchises), Crusaders, and Lumberjacks. Altogether the lack of continuity in this now prominent sport seems remarkable, given that the city is located just across the lake from the birthplace of hockey.

Yet in all of the city's Erie history, we often forget the origin of the name of the lake and all that followed. Identified as the "Cat Nation" by French missionaries in the early 1600s, the Erie, or Eriehronon, were Native Americans who lived on the southern shore of the lake that bears their name. Recent studies place them in the area between what is now Erie, Pennsylvania, and Dunkirk, New York. By the late 1600s, they had all but disappeared, the losers in a major war with the Iroquois. It was the lake that carried on their name and thereafter gave identity to all the things that make northeastern Ohio a bit "eerie" at times.

One of the 168 Veterans of the Revolutionary War, the War of 1812, the Civil War, and the Spanish-American War.

An early (1859) photograph of Erie Street Cemetery, where the dress and pose of the bystanders lend a somewhat funereal atmosphere to the image.

EUCLID

Scan to learn more

Things named Euclid abound in Cleveland—there's a street, a township, a city, and dozens of businesses (including a famous tavern on the Case Western Reserve University campus) that are, all or in part, Euclidian in name. One might suspect that the city's Greek population has had something to do with this, but the first use of the name in the region predates Greek immigration to Cleveland by nearly a century.

The name is actually a consequence of the first labor dispute to have taken place in the Western Reserve. The surveyors who accompanied Moses Cleaveland to the area in 1796 had an unbelievably difficult job—they fought heat, mosquitos, snakes, and swampy conditions as they laid out chains and stakes to measure the land. They protested, seeking more compensation. Cleaveland offered them one of the townships they had surveyed. Forty-one of them took up the offer and, at the suggestion of one of surveyors, Moses Warren, named the township after their patron, the Greek mathematician and geometrician, Euclid.

The township was only the start. Next came the road that ran from Cleveland through the township. First known as the Buffalo Road (because it eventually led to Buffalo, New York), it became known as Euclid. But what really locked the name into the local

This print, originally drawn by Thomas Whelpley in 1832, shows the Buffalo Road (Euclid Avenue) immediately east of Public Square.

historical pantheon was the fact that a section of Euclid Avenue in Cleveland developed into a fabulous residential district in the years after the Civil War. Dotted with huge mansions and spacious lawns, it became known as Millionaires' Row and was, by the 1890s, touted in travel guides as a must-see sight in Cleveland.

Today Euclid Avenue (aka the Euclid Corridor, or U.S. Route 20) still runs through to Euclid Township and eventually as Route 20 to Buffalo.

Dunham Tavern Museum, built in 1824 as a stagecoach stop on the Buffalo Road.

EUCLID BEACH

Scan to learn more

Built in 1914, Car #1218 took Clevelanders to Euclid Beach, and later from Shaker Heights to downtown Cleveland.

"At Euclid Beach on the flying turns, I'll bet you can't keep her smiling." So went one of the lines in the Beach Boys' song, "Amusement Parks USA." That line forms part of the nostalgia for a Cleveland amusement park that simply refuses to be forgotten.

Situated on the shore of Lake Erie at what is now East 156th Street, Euclid Beach was one of dozens of urban amusement parks established in the late nineteenth century around the nation. Euclid Beach, established in 1894, was modeled, in part, after Coney Island. It flourished after being sold in 1901 to the Humphrey family who made the park family-friendly by banning alcohol and unseemly amusements. In its heyday, which lasted into the 1960s, the park offered numerous rides, an arcade, a bathing beach, and a dancehall. It was the site of innumerable special days for employees of area industrial plants, businesses, and schoolchildren. It was also the site of the annual local Democratic Party steer roast. That event brought senator, and later presidential candidate John F. Kennedy to Cleveland three times. Those events attracted a huge portion of the regional population to the park and thus began a generational passing of memories that linger today. Those memories say much about what blue-collar Cleveland was like during the first seven decades of the twentieth century. Not all are pleasant. The park, like others, was racially divided—it offered special "colored days" and its dance pavilion was off limits to African Americans. Protests against the practice in 1946 resulted in a disturbance known as the Euclid Beach Riot, which, in turn, led to new local licensing laws that banned racial discrimination at amusement parks and a wider recognition in Cleveland of the need for equal access and accommodation laws. The park reopened as an integrated venue the following year.

Euclid Beach closed in 1969, a victim of changing tastes, lake pollution, racial incidents, and the rise of huge parks, such as Cedar Point, outside the urban area. Today the site of the park is marked by its landmark entrance arch. But its memory is also continued by a cadre of collectors who rescued bits and pieces of its midway and rides. "Laughing Sal," the star of the entrance to the fun house, still makes the rounds of exhibits and malls. The stainless-steel, Buck Rogers–style rocket ship cars from the aerial ride are now motorized, wheeled vehicles that can often be seen loaded with tourists on city streets during the summer. And the park's 1910 carousel is fully restored and reactivated in a special pavilion at the Western Reserve Historical Society. On any given day in Cleveland, it is inevitable that someone who remembers the park will be introducing his or her grandchild or a friend to some of the working remains of a community memory.

Francis, David, and Diane Francis. *Cleveland Amusement Park Memories*. Cleveland: Gray and Company, 2005.

The carousel at Euclid Beach, ca. 1910–1920. The original now operates at the Cleveland History Center of the Western Reserve Historical Society.

CLEVELAND A to Z

THE FLATS

Scan to learn more

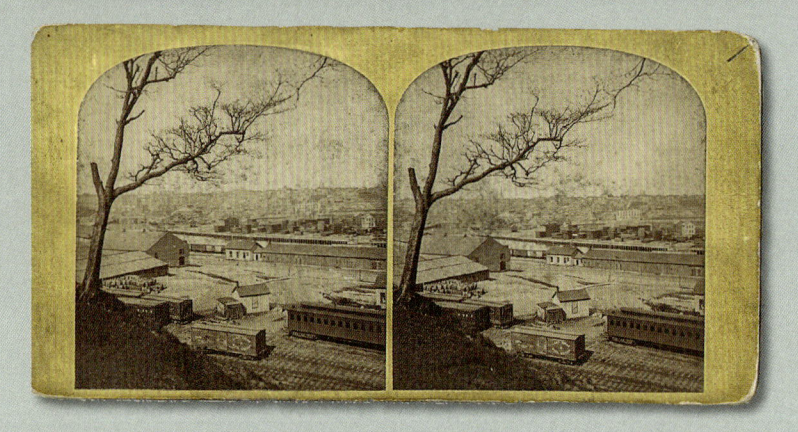

By the late 1860s, railroads and industry had already staked a claim to large areas of Cleveland's Flats.

Cleveland's Flats are both a geographical feature and a mutable symbol of the city's economy and hopes over time.

The Flats are flat—a wide flood plain that encompasses the valley of the Cuyahoga River at and near its mouth. They form an enormous divide between the East and West Sides, one which was not bridged by a high level span until the completion of the Superior Viaduct in 1878. Until then, a trip from West Side to East or vice versa involved a descent down a rather steep hill, traversing the Flats and crossing the river by a bridge that could be open or closed, depending on river traffic, and then ascending the hill on the other side.

Albeit, a divider, the Flats seemed oblivious to that role. Swampy and malarial at first, the land around the river mouth soon transformed into an area of docks and warehouses. With the coming of the Ohio and Erie Canal, which entered the city via the river valley, the Flats in the 1830s became the center for commerce, trade, and shipping. Cleveland's first railroad, which ran to Cincinnati, entered the city through the Flats, and Rockefeller's first oil refinery was situated just south of the Flats at the confluence of Kingsbury Run and the Cuyahoga. By the late nineteenth century, the Flats were all about industry—everything from paint to sewing machines. And the area remained that way into the 1960s. The Flats were dirty, smoky, noisy, and crude, but charming in all their industrial ambiance. Crooked brick streets, diverse architecture, a meandering river, and industrial urban legend helped recreate the Flats into an entertainment center in the 1970s and 1980s. As industry declined, the Flats became a symbol of Cleveland on the rebound with pleasure boats competing for river space on an increasingly cleaner Cuyahoga River.

Yet, by the early 2000s, the party was nearly over—the Flats had become rowdy and tawdry, a victim of strip clubs, cheap beer, and underage drinking. The decline, perhaps, was an echo of the dot-com collapse, or of a post-industrial return to a past of tough stevedores, thirsty mill workers, and the vices that once catered to their needs.

Today, the Flats are again being reinvented. The new East Bank project has created a city within the city at the mouth of the river. An aquarium occupies a former streetcar powerhouse, and a rowing center graces a curve in the river near Irishtown bend at Merwin's Wharf, one of the Metroparks newest sites. If you are a newcomer to Cleveland and want to understand what the city was—both in terms of its actual history and its aspiration over time—study and visit the Flats.

Today, the Flats is home to offices, hotels, condominiums, apartments, restaurants, bars, entertainment, and recreation.

20 CLEVELAND A to Z

FRANKLIN CASTLE

Scan to learn more

After years of failed starts, Franklin Castle is being restored to its original beauty.

Every Halloween, Cleveland's media focus on the history of local haunted houses. A perennial favorite is the Franklin Castle, located at 4308 Franklin Boulevard. The High Victorian Eclectic–style stone house is impressive even in its current condition (it was boarded up after a 1999 fire and is undergoing a stunning professional restoration at the time of this writing). Whether it is truly haunted is a question that remains open. That question aside, the house has other interesting stories to tell.

The Franklin Castle is a chapter in the story of German Cleveland. It was built in 1881 as the home of Hannes Tiedemann (1832–1908), who was a partner in a major wholesale grocery and liquor business and then the founder of three banking institutions in the city. Tiedemann's grand house was one of the showplaces of Franklin Avenue, a thoroughfare that was "the place to be" on Cleveland's West Side in the late nineteenth century. A number of the residents were, like Tiedemann, German or of German descent. The house was and remains testimony to the rapid upward mobility of many Germans who were, for most of the nineteenth century, the predominant immigrant community in Cleveland.

After Tiedemann died, the house largely remained "German" for a number of years. It was the headquarters for a German cultural club (the Bildungsverein Eintract), a singing society, and a German Socialist organization. The latter was indicative of the strong German involvement in the local Socialist movement. Its archives, including the newspaper *Das Echo* (1911–1918), were found in the house in the 1970s.

With all these Teutonic connections, perhaps the ghost (if there is one) is German. Hmm, could it be Karl Marx or possibly Charles Ruthenberg, one of the most noted radicals to come out of Cleveland? Born in Cleveland to German parents, Ruthenberg most likely visited the house. Maybe he left an ethereal presence behind. But if you want to find him today, go to Moscow; he along with John Reed and Big Bill Haywood are the only Americans to have been honored by the Soviet Union by burial within the Kremlin's walls.

Charles Ruthenberg, Socialist candidate for mayor, addresses a crowd near the West Side Market, ca. 1916. Ohio History Connection credit.

CLEVELAND A to Z

THEODATUS GARLICK (1805–1884)

Scan to learn more

Theodatus Garlick, a renaissance man with a most interesting name, ca. 1860.

A surname such as this simply cannot be ignored, particularly, when it belongs to one of the Renaissance men of early northeastern Ohio. Born in Vermont, Garlick migrated to the Cleveland area at the age of thirteen, joining his brother as a stonecutter and carver. Their main products were grinding wheels for gristmills and tombstones on which he carved inscriptions and decorative elements. On the side, he studied medicine with local doctors and in 1834 formalized this interest with a degree from the University of Maryland. But Garlick's artistic interests and dexterity gained precedence over his interest in medicine. While at the university, he began producing bas-relief portraits in wax. He then took his skills to Washington, where he sculpted reliefs of Henry Clay and Andrew Jackson.

These skills carried over to medicine, with Garlick becoming a skilled surgeon and a producer of medical instruments and anatomical models. Following a practice in Youngstown, he returned to Cleveland in 1853 and again augmented medical work with other interests. He was a naturalist and loved to fish; that led him to the vice presidency of the Cleveland Academy of Natural Sciences and to the creation of the nation's first artificial fish hatchery. He then wrote a book, *A Treatise on the Artificial Propagation of Certain Kinds of Fish*, which was published in 1857 and became a standard on the topic.

Garlick was still going strong at the age of seventy-five when he decided to teach himself Greek. For his next project, he translated the Bible! The Bedford Historical Society holds one of the most remarkable artifacts in the region: one of the earliest photographs taken in the Western Reserve, dating 1841. It is a self-portrait of Theodatus Garlick. Ever curious, he read about the new daguerreotype process, which had been invented in France in 1839. He then built his own camera, learned the somewhat complex chemistry for the process, and then became both photographer and subject. The portrait, like its subject, is one of a kind.

A short walk from Garlick's home is Bedford's Public Square, with memorials to Veterans of America's wars and Baseball Hall of Famer Elmer Flick.

Cleveland A to Z

GIDDINGS AVENUE

Scan to learn more

There is nothing truly historical about Giddings Avenue itself, but there are several stories in the street's past that illustrate how place and name have often shifted in Cleveland.

Giddings was named after Charles M. Giddings, an early Cleveland merchant. The street, which ran north from Woodland and terminated at Superior, had the good fortune of intersecting with Euclid Avenue, the city's Millionaires' Row. Giddings Avenue was paralleled for part of its route by Giddings Brook, one of the streams, such as Doan Brook, that was part of the south-to-north watershed emptying into Lake Erie.

Today neither the brook nor most of the street appears on contemporary maps. Giddings Avenue (except for a small segment at Wade Park) succumbed to a Progressive Era name change, typical of the rationalism of that period. It and almost every other north-to-south street in Cleveland were assigned a number in lieu of a name in 1906 (a process that has come to frustrate genealogists searching for their ancestors' residences). Starting at Public Square at Ontario, streets were sequentially numbered both east and west, and house and building numbers changed so as to reflect a property's position between the numbered streets. But some things endured—school names, for instance. Long after Giddings became part of East 71st Street, Giddings Elementary School lived on, as did Sterling school on what became East 30th Street.

The brook, like many other urban waterways, including Morgan Run and Burke Brook in the Slavic Village neighborhood, was culverted, but in the case of Giddings Brook, the stream was also diverted. Instead of running into Lake Erie, it was redirected to join Doan Brook via a storm sewer. Streams like Giddings were part of the community landscape for years—indeed, some, like Morgan and Burke Brook, created the edges of neighborhoods, but most have fully or largely disappeared.

Today it is still wise to remember both Giddings Avenue and Brook—particularly if driving along Chester Avenue. One of Cleveland's first traffic enforcement cameras (which were later declared illegal) operated at the light where Chester crosses East 71st Street. It was an ideal location for a camera because the crossing is at a substantial dip in the roadway, which increases motorists' speed. That dip is what remains of the valley of Giddings Brook!

Giddings Brook formed a pond and part of the landscape at the A. P. Winslow house near what is now East 71st and Euclid, as seen in this 1870s photograph.

The intersection of Giddings and Wade Park, showing a neighborhood in transition.

CLEVELAND A to Z

GLENVILLE

Scan to learn more

One might consider Cleveland to be a federation of neighborhoods bound together as a city. Each has a name created by early settlers or a particular ethnic community. These days, however, someone in a planning office decides just what name and what boundaries a local "hood" should have. These bureaucratic labels sometimes reference the historic names, but not often do they reflect the original boundaries as perceived by the inhabitants.

The interesting question is where the original name came from and how the "area" has been regarded over time. Glenville, which stretches north along East 105th Street beyond University Circle, is an interesting and well-known example.

Many Clevelanders know Glenville as the childhood home of Superman creators Jerry Siegel and Joe Shuster; others remember it as the site of the Glenville Shootout, an urban rebellion that took place in 1968. Glenville has been seen throughout its history as Jewish, African American, or upper class and slightly exclusive. It has been all of those. It was also the home of one of the nation's best trotting tracks (with an adjacent casino) in the late nineteenth century, and before that, like all of Greater Cleveland, it was farmland.

What many people forget or do not know is that Glenville began as an independent village that was eventually annexed into the city of Cleveland. That is not an uncommon story. When Cleveland became a village in 1815, its eastern boundary was what now East 9th Street is. It grew by annexation and many of the areas it absorbed had their own histories that linger on in neighborhood names. Ohio City, Brooklyn (now referred to as Old Brooklyn), Collinwood, Nottingham, and Corlett are communities that were annexed but still retain their neighborhood identities.

By the 1920s, growth by annexation had largely ended and a new phenomenon was in place. New communities that did not want to be part of the city were established on its periphery. Inner ring suburbs—Lakewood, Cleveland Heights, East Cleveland, and Shaker Heights—were established in the first two decades of the twentieth century. Post–World War II automotive urban sprawl completed the fragmentation. By the 1990s, 38 cities, 19 villages, and 2 townships occupied Cuyahoga County.

Despite this fragmentation of identity within the city by neighborhood and outside it by separate communities, almost all residents refer to themselves as Clevelanders. Some argue that Greater Cleveland needs to go beyond this type of personal allegiance and create a regional government. That sounds logical and it certainly might be fiscally wise, yet it has been proposed unsuccessfully since the 1930s. Perhaps we need to look to Glenville, as its identity has survived for well over a century despite being absorbed into Cleveland. Diverse peoples still relate to it even though they may have moved away. It may, however, take Jerry Siegel and Joe Shuster's "Man of Steel," who was born in Glenville (not Krypton), to convince Clevelanders of the benefits of regionalism!

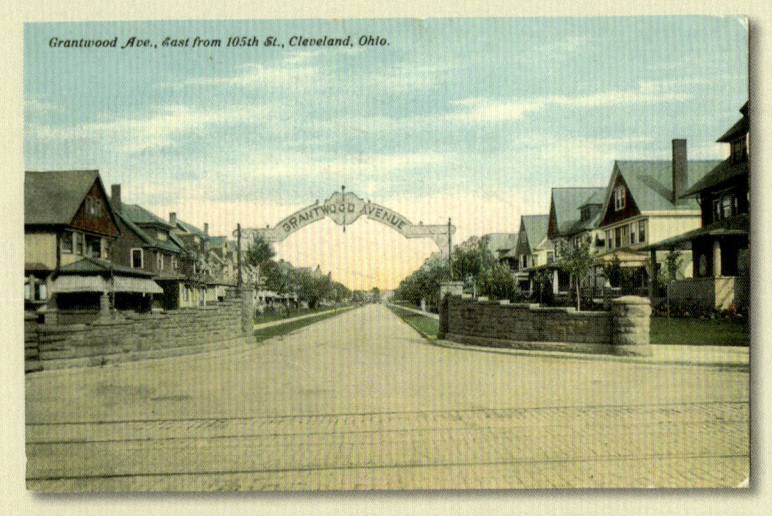

Grantwood Avenue was an up-and-coming middle-class housing development in Glenville, ca. 1910.

The "Superman House," where Jerry Siegel grew up and spent hours with Joe Shuster creating "The Man of Steel."

CLEVELAND A to Z

MARCUS ALONZO HANNA (1837-1904)

Scan to learn more

Ohio today remains a critical swing state in national political contests—as Ohio goes, so goes the nation. Yet one could argue that this electoral reputation is only a shadow of the clout the state and, particularly, Cleveland had in national affairs in the decades after the Civil War. During that period Presidents Grant, Hayes, Garfield, Harrison, McKinley, Taft, and Harding were Ohioans—with Garfield's roots in northeastern Ohio. This connection grew from the city and state's critical role in the Civil War and also because of the power and money that emanated from Gilded Age industrial Cleveland. The consummate power broker for a good part of that era was Mark Hanna of Cleveland.

Hanna arrived in Cleveland as a young man in 1852, attended the city's Central High School (John D. Rockefeller was a classmate), and then proceeded to enter business and accumulate great wealth. He worked in his family's wholesale grocery story, married into the Rhodes family, joining their coal and iron business, and upon the death of his father-in-law assumed control of the enterprise that became M. A. Hanna Co. (today's PolyOne Corp.). He also owned lucrative street railway franchises. But his real love, indeed, his forte, was political organization.

Hanna came to manage the successful campaigns of Ohioan John Sherman for Senate, Joseph Foraker for governor, and William McKinley for president in 1896, making Hanna a figure of national consequence. He was essentially the Karl Rove of the time.

The McKinley campaign was so important that Hanna absented himself from his business affairs in 1894 to begin the process of engineering McKinley's election. It was a contentious battle in a nation increasingly divided by wealth and region and just coming out of a deep recession. McKinley's opponent, William Jennings Bryan, seemed a wild-eyed radical to conservative Americans, while McKinley, a Civil War veteran, seemed to some a representative of the wealthy plutocracy that controlled business and politics. Hanna was an adept manager. He raised a war chest of an estimated $3 million to $10 million from wealthy backers and businesses and built a campaign that employed the most modern media of the age to promote Republican monetary policy and to demonize Bryan. While Bryan traveled the nation giving speeches, McKinley stayed at home in Canton, and Hanna arranged for nearly a half-million potential voters to travel to Canton in what became known as the "front porch campaign."

The strategy worked. McKinley was elected and then reelected in 1900, and in 1897 Hanna entered the U.S. Senate—a political office that seemed ideal for his demeanor and style. Some thought his next stop might be the White House, but he died in 1904.

Hanna is memorialized in Cleveland by a statue by August St. Gaudens in University Circle. He looks very senatorial, seated in a magnificent chair looking south across Euclid Avenue. Interestingly, one of his great political and business nemeses, Cleveland reform mayor Tom L. Johnson, also has a seated statue, but on Public Square. In his hand he holds a copy of Henry George's book, *Progress and Poverty*—a somewhat radical tract in the minds of people like Hanna. Fortunately, the two statues are miles apart. One can only imagine the memorial contention if they were proximate!

Hanna statue in University Circle.

Senator Marcus A. Hanna shares a carriage with Theodore Roosevelt and Myron T. Herrick, ca. 1903.

THE HARVARD CLUB

Scan to learn more

Once upon a time in Cleveland, gambling was illegal, so the best place to play the slots, roulette, or throw the dice was in a suburb outside the city. A number of venues prospered from the 1920s into the 1960s, including the Pettibone Club in Geauga County and the Mounds Club in Lake County. The Harvard Club, established in 1930, was nearer at hand, located on Harvard Avenue in Newburgh Heights. Despite its name, it was not an Ivy League alumni hangout, but a home for slots, cards, dice, and high and low rollers (the author's father among them).

Its presence in Cuyahoga County, just a short walk beyond the Cleveland city limits, was an embarrassment to local law enforcement and an affront to citizens who held fast to a Puritanical dislike of gain by chance rather than labor. Eliot Ness, Cleveland's safety director, executed a cross-border raid on the club in 1936, an event that helped buttress his reputation at the time. But the club simply moved down Harvard and

The vacant lot where the infamous Harvard Club once stood.

Eliot Ness's raid on the Harvard Club was front-page news in Cleveland in 1936.

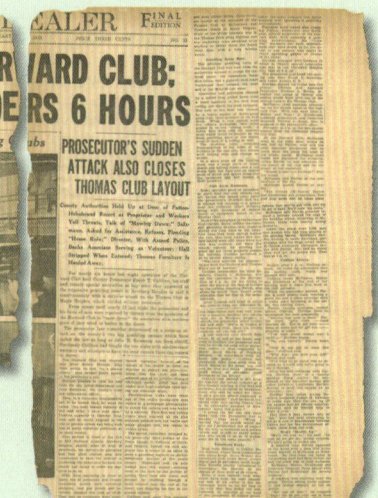

reopened. Another raid in 1941 closed it for good.

Nevertheless, gambling continued as an underground activity in and around the city. Within the city the "numbers" game flourished, its territories doled out and overseen by Alex Shondor Birns, one of the city's most famous racketeers. Among his insubordinate subordinates was Don King, who later claimed fame as a boxing promoter. Birns died violently in 1975 when he was blown apart by a bomb placed in his automobile.

Today the Birns-King numbers racket has been muscled out by the state lottery. Wheels, slots, cards, and dice are legitimate at the JACK Casino, which, ironically, sits across Public Square from Old Stone (First Presbyterian) Church, a monument to the culture and ideals of the early New England settlers whose antipathy to gambling shaped the city's attitude for well over a century. So if you choose to visit the casino, you might want to drive along Harvard Avenue. A vacant lot at 4209 Harvard occupies the site of the former Harvard Club. The trip just might enhance your chances!

Porrello, Rick. *To Kill the Irishman: The War That Crippled the Mafia.* Cleveland: Next Hat Press, 2004.

CLEVELAND A to Z

THE HEIGHTS

Scan to learn more

> **THE CLEVELAND BLUE BOOK** vii
>
> ## Shaker Village at a Glance
>
> A community of refined homes.
>
> Protection for 99 years by deed—restrictions against all controllable community offenses.
>
> Censorship of all building plans.
>
> Constant development of each section of the community without unsightly contrast in style or value of homes.
>
> Five square miles of area; forty-five miles of illumined streets; six schools in commission, and sites and plans ready for three more.
>
> Electrified, high speed transportation, built for this community, which requires but half the time of usual car service.
>
> If you want a home where your children's companions are from equally well-ordered homes—find it here. May we serve you?
>
> ## The Van Sweringen Company
> *Creators and Developers of Shaker Village*
> Fairmount 2580

The intention of exclusivity in the heights becomes readily apparent in the advertisement for Shaker Heights from a Cleveland Blue Book (social directory) from 1924.

"Moving up" in Cleveland has usually been a literal as well as figurative transition for families in search of new homes and lifestyles. It can be confusing—there are so many "Heights," including Garfield Heights, Cuyahoga Heights, Maple Heights, Cleveland Heights, University Heights, Shaker Heights, Mayfield Heights, Parma Heights, Warrensville Heights, Bedford Heights, Newburgh Heights, Broadview Heights, and Highland Heights. Some are higher in status than others but all share a common origin—the topography of Greater Cleveland. The Cuyahoga River valley allows many surrounding areas, such as Garfield Heights, Cuyahoga Heights, and Newburgh Heights, to claim an escalated status. More intriguing, however, is the fact that many of the heights suburbs sit on the shorelines of ancient predecessors to Lake Erie. The most prominent of these divides is the one East Side motorists experience when they drive up Mayfield Road, Edgehill, or Cedar Hill—they start their journeys in the lowlands of Cleveland, a former lakebed, and end up in Cleveland Heights on the shoreline of that lake. If you look closely as you drive up Mayfield Road hill, you'll notice the shale deposits of the escarpment. Other heights, such as Broadview Heights ("the highest of the heights"), are located on hills that rise on these ancient escarpments.

During the 1890s through 1920s, the residential developers of suburbs like Cleveland Heights and Shaker Heights claimed various benefits for the new locations—warmer winters, cooler summers, and freedom from the smoke and pollution of the growing industrial city below. They also implied a status shift, suggesting that those who lived in Parma Heights, for example, were a social step above those in just Parma.

Michney, Todd M. *Surrogate Suburbs: Black Upward Mobility and Neighborhood Change in Cleveland, 1900–1980.* Chapel Hill: University of North Carolina Press, 2017.

The children's playhouse on the grounds of the former Briggs Estate in Cleveland Heights.

CLEVELAND A to Z

HESSLER

Scan to learn more

Hessler Road and Hessler Court, somewhat hidden away on the Case Western Reserve University campus, are landmarks that serve as portals into different pasts.

Hessler Court, which runs from Bellflower Road to Hessler Road, is a 300-foot stretch of wooden-paved road—the last such road in Cleveland. That fact opens the question of how the city's streets were paved over time, and while that topic may seem boring at first, it does have some interesting connections. Beginning in the 1840s, Cleveland experimented with a variety of paving materials: wood planks, wood block, stone, and macadam. In the late 1880s it began to use red brick (often made from local clay deposits), which eventually became the predominant pavement.

One need not go far from Hessler Court to see a red brick pavement, as Hessler Road, which marks one of its termini, retains another piece of the communal paved past: a red brick road that very likely was laid by residents of nearby Little Italy. But there is a more interesting past to Hessler Road. It has always been an academic alley of sorts, home to artists, faculty, and students from the neighboring university for nearly a century. Those inhabitants seem to traditionally have challenged the norm; no more so than in the 1960s when Hessler Road became a small-scale version of Greenwich Village or, if you wish, Haight-Ashbury. It was about more than a "toke," however, because the Hessler mindset helped create the Cleveland Food Co-op, and the residents successfully fought off plans for redevelopment of the street by the university. They raised the funds to combat the university by holding a street fair, complete with jugglers, poets, food, and arts and crafts products. The fair continued until 1984. Then the '60s returned with a new version of the fair in 1995. It continues to this day. So if you are interested in wood or brick streets, or a "trip" back to the 1960s, stop at Hessler Road in late May for the Hessler Street Fair, where the counterculture continues in one of Cleveland's smallest, but most interesting, neighborhoods.

Case Western Reserve University students and other protestors block Euclid Avenue on May 4, 1970, at a time when Hessler Road was the center of counterculture and radicalism on the University's campus. Case Western Reserve University Archives.

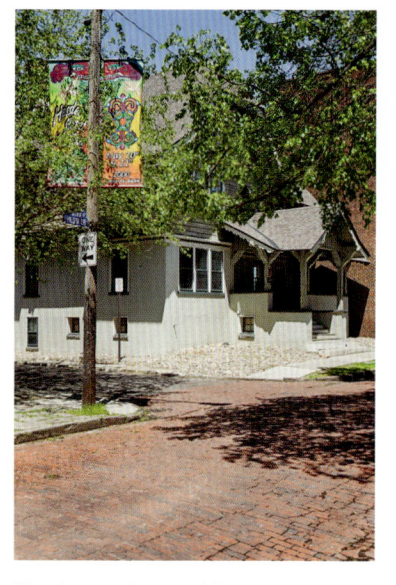

The former home of Emory Hessler occupies the intersection of Hessler Road and Hessler Court.

THE I-X CENTER

Scan to learn more

Tanks roll off the production line at the Cleveland Tank Plant, ca. 1953. Special Collections, Michael Schwartz Library, Cleveland State University.

in this somewhat unusual history lies a deeper story. The former plant was and remains a symbol of the huge industrial contribution that companies in Cleveland made to national defense during World War II and the Cold War. The war brought Cleveland fully out of the Great Depression when, at one point, unemployment was 30 percent. Between 1940 and 1944, industrial jobs rose from 191,000 to 340,000. It's not surprising, therefore, that the I-X Center is a focal point for regional industrial nostalgia—a nostalgia that is ironically appropriate at the annual auto show, given that General Motors managed bomber and tank production on the same floor many decades earlier. That the GM products at the auto show now share space with those built by "former enemies" is something else to ponder.

Albrecht, Brian, and James Banks. *Cleveland in World War II*. Charleston, SC: The History Press, 2015.

Memories and old habits tend to linger in Greater Cleveland, so it is still not unusual to hear someone of a certain age talking about going to the auto show at the Bomber Plant or seeing the Recreational Vehicle display at the Tank Plant. What they really mean is the I-X (International Exposition) Center located just outside of Cleveland Hopkins International Airport. It is one of the largest exhibition centers in the nation and annually hosts a number of shows, including the Cleveland Auto Show. But, despite its indoor Ferris wheel, it did have a previous life. It was, indeed, built (by the Department of Defense) to produce parts for bombers in 1942. Moribund during the postwar period, it came into use as a production facility for army tanks during the Korean War and then continued to produce armaments until 1972. Its current use as an exhibition hall dates from 1985. But

The 125-foot Ferris Wheel in the center of the 2.2-million-square-foot I-X Center.

CLEVELAND A to Z

JOC-O-SOT (1810–1844)

Scan to learn more

A lithograph by Day and Haghe depicts Joc-O-Sot during his visit to London in 1844.

A grave marker in Cleveland's Erie Street Cemetery hints at a part of the community's diversity that is often forgotten—that of its first peoples. While not born in Cleveland, Joc-O-Sot, or Walking Bear, was a member of the Sauk tribe who came to the city in the 1830s after the Black Hawk Wars. Black Hawk, the chief who led the Sauks in the war, purportedly came to Cleveland in the 1830s. He did so to visit his mother's grave, which reportedly was located on the west bank of the Cuyahoga on bluff where Riverside Cemetery is now located.

Those visits were reminders of the nearly ten millennia that Native Americans were resident in northeastern Ohio. Few were in the region when Moses Cleaveland arrived because the area was a type of neutral buffer zone between the Iroquois tribes to the east and the Seneca and other tribes to the west. Nevertheless, early settlers found mounds and other remains that testified to a long-standing woodland civilization that had preceded their own arrival.

As the city grew, Native Americans came and went. Numbers rose and fell, two were present in 1900, forty-eight in 1910, and thirty-four in 1920. One was Oghema Niagara (Chief Thunderwater, 1865–1950) who remained in the city until his death. He was called upon at various civic ceremonies to represent "his people." And that's how many Clevelanders saw him, at anniversaries of Moses Cleaveland's arrival and at the city's 150th anniversary in 1946. He also made an annual trip to Joc-O-Sot's grave. What most Clevelanders did not see was his activism—he provided for and sheltered other Native American migrants to the city and advocated for his community. He, like Joc-O-Sot, is buried in Erie Street Cemetery.

Oghema Niagara lived almost long enough to see a new phase of Native American history in the area. In the 1950s, the federal government urged Indians to relocate from the reservations to the city. Nearly 1,200 lived in Cleveland in 1970, mostly from western tribes. One was Russell Means, who would become head of the Cleveland American Indian Center and a prominent figure in the Indian rights movement of the 1970s. When he was asked to come to a reenactment of Moses Cleaveland's landing for the city's 175th anniversary in 1971, he did so, along with other Native Americans. Together they "greeted" Moses Cleaveland with protest signs and slogans. It was not what the planners of the event expected. It was part of a series of events locally and nationally that prompted many to reconsider their image of Native Americans. It's a change in view that continues to be debated today. The fact that Joc-O-Sot and Oghema Niagara are buried in a cemetery across the street from the city's professional baseball field should remind us who the real Cleveland Indians were.

The burial site of Joc-O-Sot in the Erie Street Cemetery.

TOM L. JOHNSON (1854–1911)

Scan to learn more

Statue of Tom Johnson by Herman N. Matzen, erected in 1915.

Tom Johnson in his 1902 Cleveland-built Winton "Red Devil" automobile.

Relatively few mayors of American cities are depicted in statuary, a rare honor not often accorded to municipal leaders. Cleveland's Tom L. Johnson, however, has two statues—one on the north side of Public Square and the other at the Western Reserve Historical Society.

This is fitting, as Johnson's mayoralty (1901–1909) is one of the aspects of the city's history that gets national historical attention. Even when he was mayor, he received broad national recognition, characterized by journalist Lincoln Steffans as "the best mayor of the best governed city in the United States." Johnson's drive to professionalize the management of the city, his advocacy of municipal ownership, and his ebullient public persona made news in the early 1900s and, indeed, transformed the city into a model for the rest of the nation. Along with President Teddy Roosevelt, and California governor Hiram Johnson, Cleveland's "Tom L." ranks among the leading reform figures in America's Progressive Era.

Beyond that, Johnson was simply a fascinating character. A self-made man, he rose from office boy to millionaire, making money in the business of running private street railways in cities such as Indianapolis, St. Louis, Brooklyn, and Cleveland. He was also an inventor, creating a fare box, an improved streetcar rail, and a working prototype for a "maglev" vehicle. He chose to move to Cleveland in 1879 and became one of the residents of Euclid Avenue, the city's Millionaires' Row. But then he had a conversion experience—not religious, but political. Johnson the plutocrat became Johnson the Progressive reformer, advocating radical measures such as the single tax on property and municipal ownership of utilities, including the private street railways, which had built his fortune.

He spent that fortune in his political campaigns, which centered on flamboyant public presentations in a tent that traveled with him and his entourage. He also spent his health on his commitment to causes such as a three-cent fare for streetcar travel. The strain of governing along with a sometimes immoderate lifestyle would damage his health; two colleagues recalled that his usual breakfast consisted of "fruit, cereal, ham and eggs, a stack of flapjacks, syrup, toast, and several cups of coffee." His loss in the mayoral campaign of 1909 was huge blow, as was his increasing loss of control within the local Democratic Party. He died two years later, his passing mourned by friend and foe alike.

If you wish to pay homage to Tom Johnson, visit his statues and see how the city chose to honor someone who challenged the status quo. If you want to visit his grave, go to Greenwood Cemetery in Brooklyn, New York. You'll find him buried next to his friend Henry George, whose book, *Progress and Poverty*, transformed Johnson from a business baron into an idealistic reformer.

KARAMU HOUSE

Scan to learn more

The home of black writer Langston Hughes, where he honed his writing skills, stands around the corner from Karamu House where he collaborated, and several of his plays premiered.

In 1915, shortly after they married, two recent graduates from Oberlin College, Russell and Rowena Jelliffe, undertook a social service mission in Cleveland that would help bridge a rapidly widening gulf between the city's white and black citizens. They started a social settlement that focused on using the arts to help immigrants and migrants accommodate themselves to their new lives in the city. At a time when segregation was becoming increasingly acceptable in the North, they opened Playhouse Settlement to all races.

That the Jelliffes had to bridge this gap is somewhat ironic given Cleveland's early history. Its New England roots made the city a center of the antislavery movement and a stop on the Underground Railroad. Cleveland was relatively tolerant—and the nearly 800 free blacks living in the city on the eve of the Civil War were relatively well integrated into the community. But some five decades later, as new black migrants came to the city, race mattered, and segregation in public facilities and even social service agencies had become common.

Playhouse Settlement succeeded despite the atmosphere at the time of its founding. In 1927 it had acquired a theater that would be named "Karamu," the Swahili word meaning a "place of enjoyment in the center of the community." Its productions were performed by integrated casts and its works were written by black and white playwrights. One of Karamu House's most notable alums was Langston Hughes, whose plays would be performed at the settlement by the Gilpin players.

In 1949, following a fire, Karamu built a new theater complex at its current location at East 89th and Quincy Avenue.

Two Karamu actors rehearse a scene from Eugene O'Neill's play *Emperor Jones*, ca. 1940.

Its reputation was enough to attract funds for rebuilding from the Rockefeller Foundation and local philanthropist Leonard Hanna Jr.

The Jelliffes, who took a chance and challenged local sentiment, retired in 1963 but remained active with Karamu and in the civil rights movement to the ends of their lives. Russell died in 1980 and Rowena in 1992. The best way to appreciate their legacy is to take in a performance at Karamu—a good suggestion is the annual holiday production of Langston Hughes's *Black Nativity*.

32   CLEVELAND A to Z

KINGSBURY RUN

Scan to learn more

If you happen to live in Shaker Heights and take the Blue or Green Line rapid downtown, you are traversing some incredibly historic territory. Part of the trip, approximately from Woodhill to the East 36th Street station, follows the route of a major tributary to the Cuyahoga River, which was the site of some of the most pivotal moments in Cleveland's history.

The Sidaway Bridge, a pedestrian suspension bridge spanning Kingsbury Run, has stood unused since it was vandalized in 1966.

To start with, the tributary was named after James Kingsbury, who came to the area in 1797. Settling near the Cuyahoga, he, like other settlers, found the site intolerable. It was swampy, rife with mosquitos, and consequently perfect for the spread of what was then known the ague, or malaria. He quickly headed out to higher ground in Newburgh Township—as did many other settlers. In fact, by 1810 Cleveland was described as a small settlement near Newburgh.

Some five decades later, Cleveland had eclipsed Newburgh, and "Kingsbury Run" played a role in that growth. Its intersection with the Cuyahoga River became the site of John D. Rockefeller's first oil refinery, which would become Standard Oil in 1870. Both the Run and the River were crucial to the refinery as they provided for easy disposal of waste in an era largely oblivious to environmental degradation.

Another fifty years later, Oris Paxton and Mantis James Van Sweringen found that Kingsbury's valley was the best possible route for light rail access to their new real estate venture, Shaker Heights. So they built their model suburb, created the light rail, and then built the Cleveland Union Terminal as both an end point for the light rail and as the city's major railway station. All the ventures were outsized, enormous, and of national consequence.

Those enormous feats of private enterprise are trumped, however, by another event, a series of twelve brutal murders between 1935 and 1938, in which the victims were dismembered with almost surgical precision. The first two victims of the Torso Murderer were found in the Run. In the ensuing years two more victims were found in the Run and another two in the Cuyahoga River. The crime, investigated by none other than Eliot Ness, remains unsolved.

This image of Kingsbury Run was taken during the initial survey for the Shaker Rapid (today's RTA Blue Line) in 1914.

Don't worry about the torsos on your rapid ride today, and don't spend too much time looking for a stream of water in the Run. You won't find it, for like so many of the Cuyahoga's urban tributaries—Walworth Run, Morgan Run, and Burke Brook—it has been largely culverted and covered over. You can, however, take a Cuyahoga River tour on the *Goodtime III* and ask the guide to show you where Kingsbury Run becomes visible just as it enters the river. Don't look for any arms or legs, but do remember this is the site where Rockefeller got truly rich.

Badal, James. *In the Wake of the Butcher: Cleveland's Torso Murders.* Kent, OH: Kent State Univ. Press, 2014.

CLEVELAND A to Z

KOSSUTH STATUE

Scan to learn more

Why does Cleveland have a public statue of the nineteenth-century Hungarian revolutionary leader Louis Kossuth? Is it because the city once had one of the largest concentrations of Hungarians outside of Budapest? Yes, in part. However, there are other reasons for the statue's existence and an interesting story as to why it is located where it is.

You can find Louis Kossuth's statue in University Circle. It is on the south side of Euclid between that street's intersections with Stearns Road and Martin Luther King Jr. Boulevard. It was erected in 1902 to commemorate Kossuth's visit to Cleveland in January 1852. Cleveland was one of the stops Kossuth made during a visit to the United States in 1851–52 to raise funds to support the struggle for Hungarian freedom from Austrian Hapsburg rule. He had been a leader in the revolution for that cause in 1848, but upon its failure he went into exile.

As a champion of democracy and freedom, Kossuth initially received a hero's welcome wherever he traveled on his American tour. His dashing style resulted in the sale of caps and other memorabilia associated with him. The manuscript text of a speech he delivered in Cleveland is now part of the Western Reserve Historical Society's collections.

There were very few Hungarians in the city in 1852, but fifty years later their numbers were substantial, and the leaders of the growing community commissioned the statue. Their intent was to erect it on Public Square, and they initially secured permission to do so. But European politics and interethnic antipathies had followed many immigrants to the city. Many in the Slovak community in Cleveland had no love for the Hungarians, or Magyars, who essentially were their overlords in Austria-Hungary. When they heard of the plan for the statue, they allied with other Slavic groups and approached the mayor, Tom L. Johnson. Their argument was clever. It did not center on interethnic discord. Rather, they suggested that if one ethnic group were permitted a statue on the Square, others would make similar requests. Given the growing number of immigrant groups in the city in the early 1900s, it was a legitimate argument. It worked. Kossuth was moved (exiled, if you will) to University Circle. Within five years, Kossuth had been joined in the Circle by a statue of Polish American Revolutionary hero Tadeusz Kosciuszko and a monument to Johann Goethe and Friedrich Schiller erected by the German community. These monuments perhaps presaged the idea for the Cleveland Cultural Gardens, which are the venue of memory for Cleveland's ethnic communities and the site where Goethe and Schiller now reside. Kossuth has remained in situ, as has Kosciuszko near the Cleveland Museum of Art.

Hammack, David, John Grabowski, and Diane Grabowski, eds. *Identity, Conflict & Cooperation: Central Europeans in Cleveland, 1850–1930*. Cleveland: Western Reserve Historical Society, 2002.

The statue of Louis Kossuth was unveiled in University Circle in 1902 at which time it stood immediately adjacent to the southeast section of the "circle" roadway.

The Kossuth statue is located across Euclid Avenue from the Marcus Hanna statue.

LAKE VIEWS

Scan to learn more

Eleanor Roosevelt views the Lakeview Terrace housing complex upon its dedication in 1937. The Ernest J. Bohn Papers in the Kelvin Smith Library Special Collections, Case Western Reserve University.

Clevelanders who live near the lake know where they are in the world—every global map depicts the Great Lakes. Simply look and you can easily find Cleveland. Add to that somewhat cooler summers at the lakeshore and spectacular views, particularly sunsets, and you have a magic combination for seeking residence somewhere close to Lake Erie.

The most common lake views are those gained from homes and high rises along the shore. Whether on Lakewood's Gold Coast, at Bratenahl Place, or in an apartment on Euclid's shoreline, the views are wonderful—but then, of course, the cost for the view usually rises according to one's location in the building; north views and upper floors come at a price. Lakeside homes carry the same escalated price and, depending on the direction of wave action, the risk of losing a back yard.

Two places that have both "lake" and "view" in their name do not fit the above model. One is a pioneer public housing estate and the other the city's most notable cemetery. While their somewhat divergent histories do relate to a view, those histories also reflect on important aspects of Cleveland's past.

The cemetery is, of course, Lake View Cemetery. Its monuments, mausoleums, and landscaping are a visitor attraction. Indeed, Lake View, is one of Cleveland's finest museums, albeit an outdoor one situated in an arboretum. Established in 1869, the cemetery is the resting place of President James A. Garfield as well as many of the former residents of Euclid Avenue's Millionaires' Row and industrialists and businesspeople, including John D. Rockefeller, who transformed the city in the nineteenth and twentieth centuries. These are the graves that visitors often seek out, all while enjoying incredible views of the city and lake from various vantage points on the grounds (the best being the upper terrace of the Garfield Monument).

The other lake view is west of the river. It is Lakeview Terrace, an architecturally significant, pioneer public housing estate created during the Great Depression. Situated on a rise at the foot of West 28th Street and constructed between 1935 and 1937, Lakeview was one of the first public housing projects authorized by the federal government. Many of its units have views of the lake. It reflects another part of Cleveland's history: the city's role creating public housing during the 1930s. The primary advocate for public housing was Ernest J. Bohn, an immigrant who came to the United States from Hungary at age ten and whose political affiliation was Republican. Visiting Lakeview can cause one to reassess conceptions of public housing and politics.

The same is true for Lake View Cemetery. In this case, if you ignore the view and the grand monuments and focus on the smaller plots, you will discover the diversity that built the cemetery and the city. Lake View is the resting place of a good number of Italians, many from nearby Little Italy, who worked on its grounds and carved its monuments—as well as individuals of a variety of faiths and races. It is a sampler of the incredible mixture of people who came to live and work on the shore of the lake one sees in the distance.

The view from the hilltop across Lake View Cemetery to Lake Erie in the distance.

CLEVELAND A to Z

LEAGUE PARK

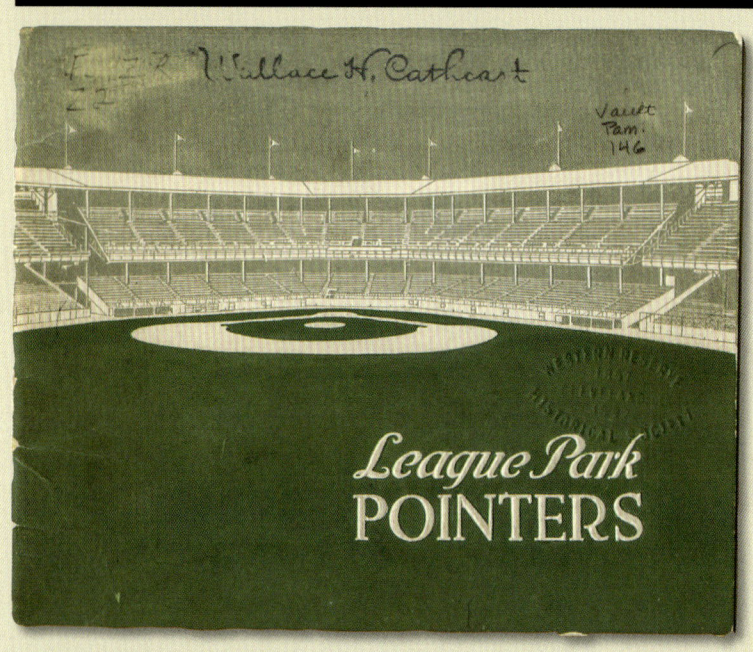

Scan to learn more

This 1914 guide to League Park provides the reader with sight lines in the park as well as ticket prices and other details.

Cleveland once had its equivalent of Fenway Park and Wrigley Field—a tight little ballpark embedded within an urban neighborhood known as Hough. Those who saw ballgames at League Park remember an intimate stadium (it accommodated 22,500 at its maximum) with unique field dimensions: the left field fence was 375 feet from the plate; center, a whopping 420 feet; and right field, 290 feet. It was paradise for a left-handed hitter. When Babe Ruth hit his 500th homerun on August 12, 1929, it was "out of the park," landing on Lexington Avenue, the street that bordered the park on the south. Ruth wanted the ball and gave twenty dollars and another autographed ball to the young boy who retrieved it.

Ruth's homerun was one of the many highlights at the park, which opened in 1891. It hosted the first Indians World Series appearance (and victory) in 1920 and the first professional game pitched by a young Bob Feller. League Park was also home to the Cleveland Buckeyes, the city's Negro League World Series champions in 1945, and to the city's first truly viable professional football team, the Rams.

By the late 1940s League Park was obsolete—too small to hold the growing crowds following Cleveland Indians baseball, not equipped with lighting for night games, and providing inadequate parking. The team ceased using the park in 1947, moving its entire schedule to the Municipal Stadium on the lakefront, a venue the Indians had used on a part-time basis since 1931. When the Indians again won the World Series in 1948 (the second and last time they did so), all the home games had been played at the new stadium. The fifth game of that contest attracted 86,288 fans to the lakefront—almost four times the capacity of the old field.

The park languished, most of its stands being demolished in 1951. But for a while, sport lived on. The Cleveland Browns used it as a practice field before moving to old Finnegan Field on the Case Western Reserve Campus in the 1960s.

Today the Park has been restored. The old ticket office at the corner of Lexington and East 66th Street, the only substantive remaining piece of the earlier structure, now houses a museum. And the actual field of dreams has been recreated with artificial turf. One can stand at the exact site where the Bambino launched his 500th home run. Or run the bases where Sam "the Jet" Jethro of the Cleveland Buckeyes and Bob Feller played the great American game, albeit in separate leagues, but with equal passion. The rebirth of League Park is not simply about memories; it is an example of the rebirth and commitment to the historic Hough Neighborhood.

The view from the batter's box. After years of neglect, League Park has undergone a thorough facelift.

LITTLE ITALY

Every year in the four days surrounding August 15th, it seems that half the population of northeastern Ohio comes to the crossroad of Mayfield and Murray Hill to celebrate the Feast of the Assumption. The festival celebrating this important Roman Catholic holiday is a must-see event for many Clevelanders, and the neighborhood, Little Italy, in which it occurs has become one of the go-to places in Cleveland. But the Little Italy of today, crowded with restaurants, art galleries, and an increasing number of upscale condos and apartments, is not the Little Italy of old.

That community began to grow in the mid-1880s, coalescing around jobs at the adjacent Lake View Cemetery. The earliest settlers, including the founder of the neighborhood, Joseph Carabelli, were stonecutters who made monuments for the cemetery. Those who followed, largely from the province of Cambobasso, also found jobs as groundskeepers in the cemetery or in industries built along the rail line that defines the community's western border. By the early 1900s it was one of the most solid immigrant neighborhoods in Cleveland, with over 90 percent of its population having been born in Italy. It was a self-contained community—many of the restaurants, shops, and galleries in today's Little Italy occupy spaces that were once groceries, butcher shops, dry goods stores, hardware stores, and other businesses that served the original residents. Although many of the structures that form the streetscape along Mayfield and Murray Hill Roads remain structurally as they were, their repurposing obscures much of the original feel of the neighborhood. Even though clad in modern siding, the residences on the back streets still give the feel of a crowded immigrant community. Look closely and you will find houses behind houses and small shotgun houses that once housed large families or groups of relatives. However, while people who have a long history on the hill occupy some houses, many others are now rented to graduate students from neighboring Case Western Reserve University.

One of the most powerful symbols of what the "Hill" was and how it came to be are the red bricks that form the paving of Murray Hill Road. Never covered with asphalt, they tell a story about Italian immigration, for many who came to live on the Hill helped Cleveland build its urban infrastructure during the early 1900s, including the laborious process of laying down brick streets such as Murray Hill. It is their monument, so to speak, as are the actual monuments they carved, including John D. Rockefeller's, in Lake View Cemetery. They also carved their own monuments at Lake View. When you next visit Lake View, look beyond the wealthy and famous buried there and you will find the resting places of many of those who once lived on the Hill.

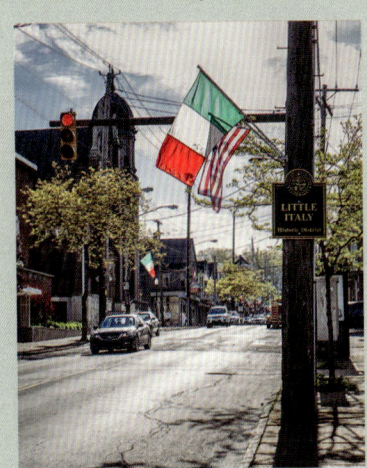

Little Italy street scene, looking east on Mayfield Road.

The railroad bridge, which today demarks the "entry" to Little Italy, was built in the early 1910s to eliminate a very busy and dangerous grade crossing at Mayfield Road.

THE MALL

Nowadays it can be confusing when someone begins a conversation about going to the mall. It could be a reference to a forthcoming shopping excursion or, perhaps, to something more substantive, such as the large open green space just northeast of Public Square.

Cleveland's Mall is a significant historic landmark and, more importantly, an example of an urban renewal plan that works. Even a century after its conception, the Mall continues to be renewed—without betraying its original concept.

That concept was simple: open a vast esplanade of green space in the center of the city and surround it with civic buildings, all similar in style and height. Its model was the order and beauty of the structures at the 1893 Columbian Exposition in Chicago, and its architectural proponents—Daniel Burnham, Arnold Brunner, and John Carrere—were three of the nation's most visionary planners. Conceived in 1902, approved in 1903, the Mall, or Group Plan as it is also known, brought national attention to Cleveland. A not inconsiderable side benefit was that the Mall replaced a squalid urban area, part of which housed one of the city's main red-light zones. Yet, as was the case with other urban renewal projects, those who had once called the area their home had to struggle to find new places to live.

By 1930, the 500-foot-wide Mall, which stretched from Superior north to the lake, was Cleveland's civic center bordered by the Federal and Cuyahoga County courthouses, Public Auditorium, City Hall, the Cleveland Public Library, and the headquarters of the Board of Education—all excepting the last, constructed in a harmonious Beaux-Arts style. One major component was missing—a railroad station that was to have been built between the County Court House and City Hall at the north end. That station ended up on Public Square.

The plan survived that change and it also accommodated itself to important additions—Marshall Fredericks's War Memorial Fountain and an underground convention center were added in the 1960s. In the 1990s a garage was built beneath the fountain, and in 2013, the Mall "rose" in part to allow construction of an enlarged convention center linked to the Global Center for Health Innovation located on the western side of the green space. Through all of this, the site has remained a visionary landmark for the city, which evidences its aspirations at the turn of two centuries—the twentieth and the twenty-first.

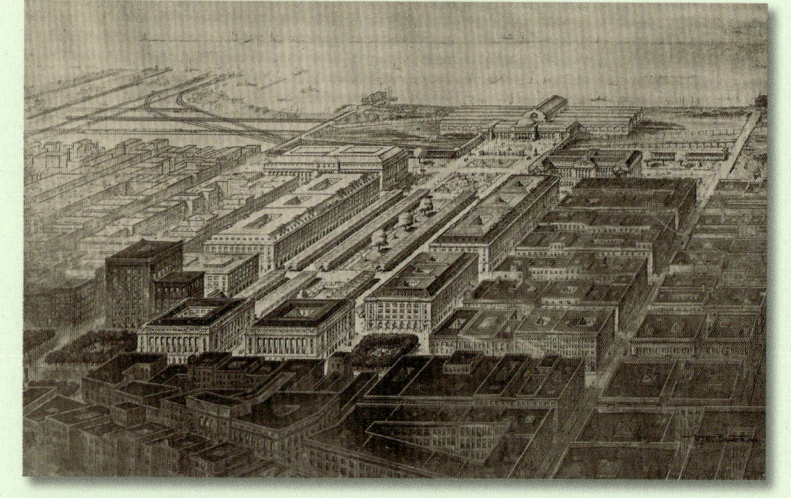

Johannesen, Eric. *Cleveland Architecture 1876–1976.* Cleveland: Western Reserve Historical Society, 1979.

Kerr, Daniel R. *Derelict Paradise: Homelessness and Urban Development in Cleveland, Ohio.* Amherst: Univ. of Massachusetts Press, 2011.

This original concept drawing for the Mall shows the grandeur of a vision that was largely achieved.

Peace Arising from the Flames of War, **with the Huntington Bank Building in the background.**

MOONDOG CORONATION BALL

A reproduction of the original promotional poster for the Moondog Coronation Ball outlines an extensive musical program that was cut short by crowds and disorder.

The Moondog Coronation Ball was not much of a ball—it ended after one song was played. But it was a coronation of sorts, for because of it, Cleveland was eventually crowned the home of rock and roll. The ball was planned by Alan Freed, a local disc jockey who had begun playing R&B music during his radio program in Akron. He did so at the suggestion of Leo Mintz, the owner of Record Rendezvous in Cleveland. Mintz had noticed an uptick in sales of black R&B music among white customers in the late 1940s. Freed moved to station WJW in Cleveland in 1951 and began a late-night program: "The Moondog Rock and Roll House Party." The music, energized by his radio persona, built a huge audience of white and black youths. He and partner Lew Platt had held smaller events, but the Moondog was to be their first major rock concert.

It could have been a huge success, but it was too huge—tickets were oversold and the resulting crowd ended up breaking down the doors at the venue and started fights within. The police were called and the show stopped after only one number—the first rock concert seemed to have set a precedent for many to follow! It also garnered huge publicity, almost all negative, but that only served to build interest in the music and the leitmotif of rebellion that has helped sustain it over the years.

Perhaps the irony of the first rock ball rests on its location. It took place in the Cleveland Arena, the city's primary venue for ice hockey and basketball, located at 3717 Euclid Avenue, formerly the site of one of the street's most famous mansions. Built by inventor (arc lamp and dynamo) Charles F. Brush, the mansion featured a huge pipe organ with pipes extending up through three floors. Undoubtedly, the music was fine and Brush's guests always behaved themselves and the police never had to intervene.

If you want to pay homage to Freed or curse him, go visit the site. The headquarters of the Cleveland branch of the American Red Cross now occupies the land where the Moondog Ball helped make rock and roll famous—and infamous—at the same time.

Adams, Deanna R. *Rock 'n' Roll and the Cleveland Connection.* Kent, OH: Kent State Univ. Press, 2002.

The jukebox marks Alan Freed's final resting place in Lakeview Cemetery.

GARRETT MORGAN (1877–1963)

Scan to learn more

Inventor Garrett Morgan is joined by his son and grandson as he poses next to a prototype of his traffic signal.

Commuters using the West Shoreway in Cleveland have a twice-daily encounter with a reminder of three seminal aspects of the city's history: water, inventive entrepreneurship, and race. All are represented by the Garrett A. Morgan Water Treatment Plant at West 45th Street and the lake shore.

Cleveland has never really had to worry about a water supply, given its location on Lake Erie. However, as it industrialized in the nineteenth century, it needed to be concerned about the quality of the water. The Cuyahoga River and the lake became increasingly polluted in the years after the Civil War. In 1856, the city's first reservoir was fed by a pipe that drew water from 300 feet offshore. By century's end, pollution had fouled all of the area around the mouth of the river and a good deal of the shoreline. Water intakes moved farther into the lake. Workers dug tunnels extending over 26,000 feet under the lake to connect pumping stations on both the East and West Sides to intakes situated in deeper and relatively clean areas of the lake.

It was hard and dangerous work. In July 1916 tunnel workers hit a pocket of natural gas that exploded, killing eleven men. The gas prevented would-be rescuers from entering—that is, all but Garrett A. Morgan, an African American inventor. The breathing hood he had invented allowed him, his brother Frank, and two other men to enter the tunnel, rescue two men, and remove four bodies before the effort was halted by officers from the U.S. Bureau of Mines.

Today Morgan is one of the heroes of Cleveland's history. Along with the breathing device, he also invented an early traffic signal with an innovative cautionary position as well as a hair relaxer that helped make him relatively wealthy. But Morgan's current fame as Cleveland's black Thomas Edison, obscures the fact that he had to struggle to gain recognition for his heroism in the tunnel disaster. Others on the team were immediately honored. His recognition came only a year later when local citizens presented him with a special medal. Morgan knew that his race was a liability in Cleveland in the 1910s, and for that reason his recognition was belated. But Morgan did not accept the status quo. He argued for the recognition he deserved. His papers at the Western Reserve Historical Society tell the tale of his struggle for recognition as well as his inventive drive. The water treatment plant that now bears his name is a fitting monument to him as well as a reminder of deeper stories in the city's history.

The Filtration House at the Garrett A. Morgan Water Treatment Plant, formerly the Division Avenue Pumping and Filtration Plant.

MUSTARD

Scan to learn more

Ballpark and Stadium mustards squaring off for the "Mustard War."

Mustard has nothing to do with the agricultural history of Cleveland and northeastern Ohio. There never was a time when immense fields of mustard glowed golden yellow in the late summer sun. Yet mustard is central to regional nostalgia—sports nostalgia to be specific. While rooted in nostalgia, the story of sports and mustard in Cleveland can be contentious. For decades the mustard provided at baseball and football games in Cleveland has been brown, not yellow, and for decades there have been two varieties: Bertman Original Ballpark Mustard and Stadium Mustard. There is constant argument as to which is superior and which was spread on the hotdog at that special game at the old Municipal Stadium.

Bertman was first served in the 1930s and until the 1970s came only in the large jugs used at the vending stands. It then made its way into supermarkets in smaller bottles. But by that time (1969), it had been joined by Stadium Mustard as a consumer product. Today Stadium Mustard has what amounts to "spreading or squirting" rights at over 150 sports venues in the United States. In Cleveland, Stadium is served at Browns games at First Energy Field, and Bertman remains in the ballpark at Progressive Field.

This early 1950s Cleveland Indians scorecard features an advertisement for the mustard familiar to generations of Cleveland baseball fans—it was always part of the game.

CLEVELAND A to Z

41

ELIOT NESS (1903–1957)

Scan to learn more

Cleveland is not Chicago—but then, one of the most famous figures in the Windy City's history became, arguably, equally famous in Cleveland. Eliot Ness, the college-educated G-man credited with helping send Al Capone to jail, arrived in Cleveland in 1934 to head the government's alcohol tax unit for northern Ohio. Within a year, newly elected mayor Harold H. Burton appointed Ness as the city's safety director. His job (a perennial one in any big city) was to clean up a corruption-plagued police department and modernize both it and the fire department.

That he did, forming a group of "Untouchables" to ferret out police who were "on the take." In one notable instance, Ness moved in to close an after-hours club. A young man at the door, not recognizing Ness, told him that the operation was OK, because the owner, his father, was a cop.

Together Burton and Ness ably managed Cleveland during the difficult years of the Depression. The police force and the fire department modernized; the city hosted the 1936 Republican National Convention; and in 1936–1937, Cleveland's Great Lakes Exposition brought millions to its lakefront site. A Republican mayor in a Democratic city, Burton was popular and served three terms before he moved to the U.S. Senate. In 1945 he gained appointment to the U.S. Supreme Court.

Ness, however, was less successful in the long run. He was frustrated in his efforts to find and arrest the culprit responsible for the Torso Murders, which occurred between 1935 and 1938. He resigned as safety director in 1942 and worked again for the feds—this time heading the Division of Social Protection during World War II. He returned to Cleveland and in 1947 ran unsuccessfully for mayor.

Ness died before he became the celebrity he is today. The book, *The Untouchables*, by Oscar Fraley came out just after his death, followed by the television series and movie that made him an American icon.

You can "find" Eliot Ness in various Cleveland locations today. A memorial honors him near the lake in Lake View Cemetery into which his ashes were scattered; the Great Lakes Brewing Company celebrates him with a Vienna Lager named in his honor—an interesting tribute to a G-man who liked to drink when, of course, it was legal; and the scrapbooks he kept to chronicle his career in Cleveland are a prized part of the Western Reserve Historical Society's collections.

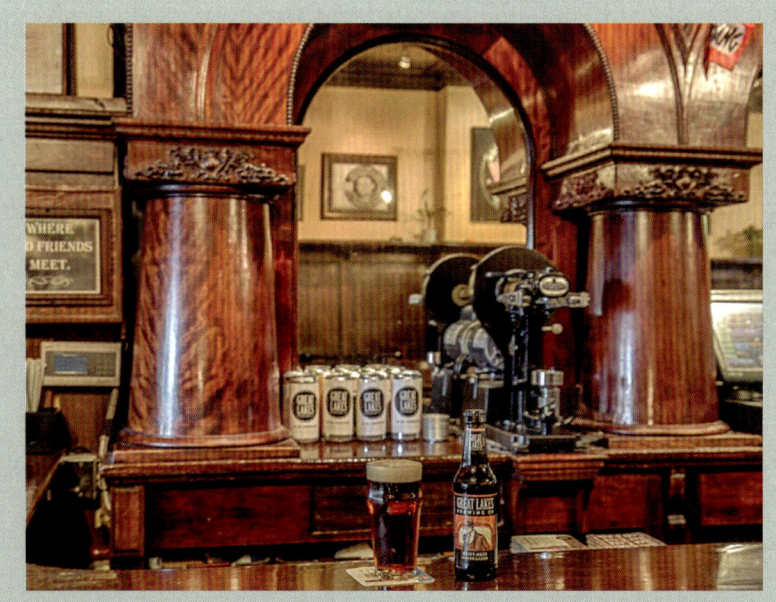

"Bang" marks the spot of one of three bullet holes at Ohio City's Market Tavern, once frequented by Eliot Ness.

Francis E. Sweeney, the man many consider the chief suspect in the Torso Murders, taunted Eliot Ness with a series of five postcards he sent to the former safety director in the mid-1950s.

CLEVELAND A to Z

OHIO CITY

Scan to learn more

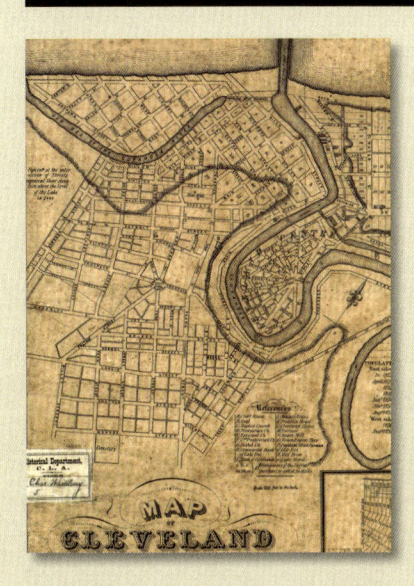

This section of an 1835 map provides an excellent overview of Ohio City's street plan.

In many ways Ohio City reveals the facts and fallacies of the East-West divide in Cleveland. For many years Ohio City was a place apart, both physically and legally from Cleveland, yet in recent decades it has become one of the most visible and vital symbols of the city.

The East-West divide predates Ohio City and it rests upon the original "ownership" of the area by Native Americans. Defeated at the Battle of Fallen Timbers, Native Americans in 1795 signed the Treaty of Greenville, which ceded their ownership of the lands east of the Cuyahoga River. That opened the East Side to survey and settlement in 1796. Ownership and legal settlement of the lands west of the river occurred nine years later when the Treaty of Fort Industry was signed. Surveys of the land then created separate townships east (Cleveland) and west (Brooklyn) of the river.

While Cleveland grew slowly—it had only 606 inhabitants in 1820—the West Side of the river was even more sparsely populated. At that point, no one truly cared about east or west. By 1827, matters changed when the first segment of the Ohio and Erie Canal opened between Cleveland and Akron and spurred lakeside economic growth. The canal ended on the East Side of the Cuyahoga River and thus gave a distinct advantage to Cleveland, but speculators sensed opportunity on the west bank as well. By the 1830s Cleveland and the "City of Ohio" were economic competitors (see The Bridge War) separated by a river and unflattering perceptions of each other. They existed side by side until 1854, when Cleveland absorbed Ohio City but remained apart because of the river and the Flats.

Even after high-level bridges began to span the valley in the late 1800s, the perception of difference continued. "Downtown" was in Cleveland, as was Millionaires Row, which overshadowed similar but smaller elite residential areas that developed along Franklin Avenue. University Circle would grow on the East Side, despite the fact that Cleveland's first university was established in 1851 in what is now the Tremont neighborhood. Cleveland's Jewish community settled and expanded on the East Side, even though its first cemetery on Willett Street was west of the river. African American settlement was largely east of the river, even though one of the first settlers west of the Cuyahoga was George Peake, an African American. Reversing the directional equation is the West Side Market, which today is considered the premier market in Cleveland, an accolade that obscures the fact that most East Siders had, for decades, done their shopping at the Sheriff Street and Central markets just south of downtown.

The differences between East and West, both trivial and consequential, remain matters of debate and discussion. Yet, Ohio City played a role in blurring those perceptions when, during the 1960s, preservationists discovered its rich architectural heritage and began to make it a chic destination for East and West Siders alike. Some thirty years later the same transformation would take place in Tremont. The irony today is that many debates over East and West now take place in bars, restaurants and clubs west of the river—places that were unreachable, or terra incognita for East Siders for much of the community's history.

Wheeler, Robert. *Pleasantly Situated on the West Side.* Cleveland: Western Reserve Historical Society, 1980

A public art project on Ohio City's Franklin Boulevard, between St. Herman's House of Hospitality and Franklin Castle.

CLEVELAND A to Z

JESSE OWENS (1913–1980)

Scan to learn more

Jesse Owens was given a triumphal victory parade when he returned to Cleveland after the 1936 Berlin Olympics.

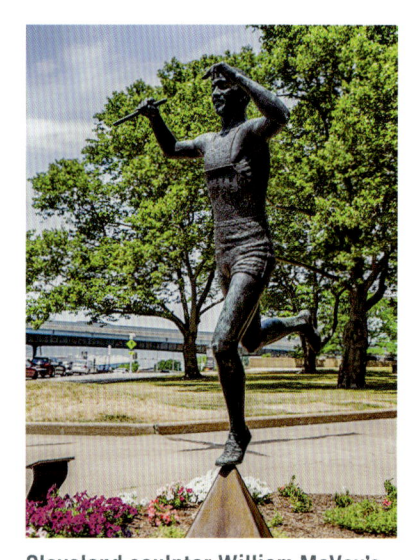

Cleveland sculptor William McVey's statue of Jesse Owens, on Fort Huntington Park.

There are arguably only a few Clevelanders or individuals with Cleveland connections whose names are readily recognizable outside of the city and the nation. Bob Hope and John D. Rockefeller rank high on this list, as does Jesse Owens. His four Olympic gold medals in the 1936 Berlin Olympics made him an international figure at the time; but what gave him an enduring legacy is the fact that he, as an African American, achieved that feat at an event tainted by the racial theories of the Third Reich.

Owens's athletic legacy began at Fairmount Junior High School near Cleveland's University Circle where coach Charles Riley perceived his talent and nurtured it. Owens became a star athlete at Cleveland's East Technical High School and then claimed collegiate glory at the Ohio State University. His athletic feats are legend, but they derived from and illustrated a broader story of Cleveland during the 1920s and 1930s.

Owens was part of the Great Migration, the movement of African Americans from the South to northern industrial cities in late nineteenth and early twentieth centuries. In search of work and freedom, they came north in enormous numbers. Cleveland had a black population of just over 2,000 in 1880. By 1930 it was just below 72,000. Among that 72,000 were Owens's family, who had come to the city from Alabama in 1922. They, like many other migrants, discovered that freedom and opportunity could be elusive in the supposedly liberal north. Cleveland, which had been a relatively tolerant, antislavery community in the years before the Civil War, had become segregated and far less tolerant of racial difference by the 1930s. Owens's athletic prowess was a point of pride for his community, and his victory at Berlin made him an American hero. Yet acceptance was only partial, and in the years after the Olympics Owens struggled against bias in his adopted hometown and the nation. By World War II, he had moved from Cleveland and began to build a solid career in jobs related to athletics and recreation.

One can argue that much had changed by 1980, the year Owens died at his home in Tucson. Cleveland, for example, had elected its first African American mayor, Carl Stokes, some thirteen years later. Yet, the city was in many ways still divided, and it remains so today. Nevertheless, Owens remains a hero in the city, something which becomes doubly appropriate when we remember that Jesse, known as "J. C.," was actually named James Cleveland Owens. Visit his statue in Fort Huntington Park at Lakeside and West 3rd Street and remember who he was and what he still represents.

PARMA

Scan to learn more

Parma, a western suburb of Cleveland, was first settled in 1816. Today it is the state's seventh largest city. Its growth occurred primarily after World War II, when it became, in some ways, a regional Levittown with many similarly styled suburban houses built quickly to fill the postwar demand for housing that was affordable and distant from the congestion of the city. Parma became a blue-collar suburb, filled with first- and second-generation Poles, Germans, Italians, Ukrainians, Irish, and other groups who were moving up. Given these origins, it typically gets little respect and has been the brunt of jokes, many of which were "insider" takes on the community. One 1960s late-night local TV movie series, "Shock Theater," hosted by Ernie Anderson, featured a filler short soap opera titled "Parma Place," which pilloried the city as ethnic and unsophisticated. It was admittedly tongue-in-cheek, but the B-grade production created a perception that continues today.

Yet those who have made light of Parma have made the mistake of comparing blue-collar recreation with high culture; affordable housing with expensive stylish homes; and dismissing foodways (see Pierogies) that seemed too plain to be respected. What they missed is that Parma, in many ways, is a continuation of the story of the Greatest Generation, as characterized by journalist Tom Brokaw—those who went through the Depression and then served in the armed forces during World War II. Upon their return to the States, they used the benefits of the GI Bill and the booming postwar economy to "move up." Parma, and other similar blue-collar suburbs such as Maple Heights, Euclid, and Garfield Heights, grew almost exponentially during this period, figuring into their image as part of the realization of the "American dream."

Visiting Parma today is a good way to see a landscape that still records the styles and aspirations of American suburbia in the 1950s and 1960s. Taken at the right time, that trip will get you to certain ethnic festivals held in the city's Polish and Ukrainian villages, festivals that had their American origins in neighborhoods such as Tremont and Slavic Village before they, too, followed America to the suburbs.

Homes in the West 44th Street neighborhood of Parma.

This 1953 aerial view of Parma Heights (near the intersection of Pearl Road and West 130th) shows this suburban area at a time when it and Parma were undergoing a huge period of growth.

CLEVELAND A to Z

45

PEERLESS

Scan to learn more

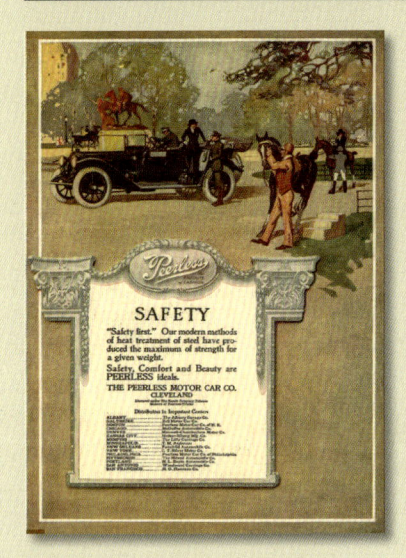

This 1914 ad is as elegant as the product it promoted, the Cleveland-built Peerless Automobile.

There are many interesting stories of what one might call "industrial evolution" in Greater Cleveland. One that deserves attention is the story of the Peerless Motor Car Company.

When established in 1889, Peerless produced washing machine wringers. Within ten years it was producing bicycles, and by 1901 it was making automobiles and automobile parts. The shift from bicycles to autos was common in the early auto industry—and at the time Peerless got into cars, northeastern Ohio had become, arguably, the automobile manufacturing capital of the nation. Between the 1890s and 1930s, the region was home to over 100 automakers. Some lasted only for a year or two, but others like Jordan, Winton, Stearns, Baker, and White, had long productive histories, helping to shape the modern automobile.

Peerless was one of the influential survivors. It produced expensive, high-end touring cars that, in terms of construction and style, lived up to the company's name—they were largely without peer. By the late 1920s this large, expensive product was going out of style. Despite experiments with less expensive and trendier models, sales lagged, and with the beginning of the Depression it became clear that a change in product was needed.

James A. Bohannon, the company president stopped auto production in 1931 and two years later decided to use the factory on Quincy Avenue for a new venture—beer. Bohannon knew that the new president, Franklin D. Roosevelt, would advocate the repeal of prohibition, the "noble" experiment that had become increasingly unpopular throughout the nation. When the time came, the Carling Brewing Company of Canada had converted the factory to a brewery. The plant on Quincy Avenue continued to produce "suds" until 1984. Its site is now occupied by the Cuyahoga County Juvenile Justice Center.

Today the Peerless legacy lives on in the Crawford auto collection of the Western Reserve Historical Society. The society holds several Peerless models, including the last one built—a rare, largely unrestored 1932 all-aluminum sedan. It was the last car to be fully built in Cleveland and is one of the treasures of the Crawford.

If you are more interested in the product that followed the '32 Peerless, you can still find a bottle of Carling Black Label, which is now brewed by Miller, or you can choose from a large number of local craft beers, for now Cleveland is one of the leaders in this burgeoning industry—just as it was in the early auto industry. But, don't drink and drive—only James Bohannon could successfully mix autos and alcohol.

The 1932 Peerless Sedan was the end of an era both for Peerless and for Cleveland. In the Crawford Auto Aviation Collection, Western Reserve Historical Society.

THE PERILS OF SOCIETY

Scan to learn more

In 1914 the film serial *Perils of Pauline* caught the nation's attention; two years later, Cleveland produced its own "perils" film—not a serial, but a melodrama in which members of Cleveland's prominent families essentially played themselves.

With direction and camera work by Katherine Bleecker (considered the earliest "moving camera woman") and Charles Darling, *Perils of Society* takes viewers to the places and events frequented by the city's elite—golf at the country club, a fox hunt in the Chagrin Valley, the Union Club, the Gwinn estate in Bratenahl, and yachting on Lake Erie. It also goes a bit down market as the homegrown actors take in a ballgame at League Park. It was all for a good cause. Screened at the Metropolitan Theater (the venue today for the Agora) in June 1916, the film served as a benefit to raise money for French war orphans. It was reputedly the second film to be produced in the city. Was Cleveland on its way to becoming the Hollywood of the Midwest? No—although viewing films at neighborhood theaters and at the grand theaters of Playhouse Square would become a major business in the city from the 1910s through the 1950s, no one then could imagine the city and the region as a production hub for America's dream factories.

Cut to the twenty-first century—the plot has changed. Cinema is big business in Cleveland, and the city is now frequently a set for major Hollywood films and a variety of regional and local productions. The creation of a state film bureau in 1976 and, importantly, a state tax incentive passed in 2009 have spurred production in Cleveland. And watching film has moved to another level. The Cleveland International Film Festival, begun in 1977, is now one of the major festivals in North America, and the Cleveland Cinematheque at the Cleveland Institute of Art has been showing classics and art films since 1984.

Yet when it's lights, camera, and action in the city, Cleveland is often playing another role—a stand-in for New York, Washington, or other urban areas. It's simple: the built urban landscape of the city, the economics of filming, and the "ease" of closing major thoroughfares make the city an ideal and more affordable locale. Severance Hall stood in for the presidential palace of Kazakhstan in the 1997 film *Air Force One*, and the Crawford Auto Aviation Museum at the Cleveland History Center became a part of the Smithsonian Institution for *Captain America: The Winter Soldier*.

Top billing, though, still comes about. The city (and the 1948 World Series champion Cleveland Indians) starred in *The Kid from Cleveland* (1949), and the Cleveland Browns and 10,000 stand-in fans were a big part of the *Fortune Cookie* (1966). More recently, Clevelanders Anthony and Joe Russo produced *Welcome to Collinwood* (2002) in various city locales. The film would launch their career, and it would be the Russos who would guide Captain America to the city twelve years later.

It's doubtful that the amateurs who acted in *Perils* envisioned a sequel or saw themselves as pioneers. But in one sense they were—early on they realized films could make money (in their case, for a good cause), and they knew the city had some great backdrops. *Perils* is a gem of a movie. If you want to catch the film, check it out at the Western Reserve Historical Society where a copy is preserved and DVDs are for sale.

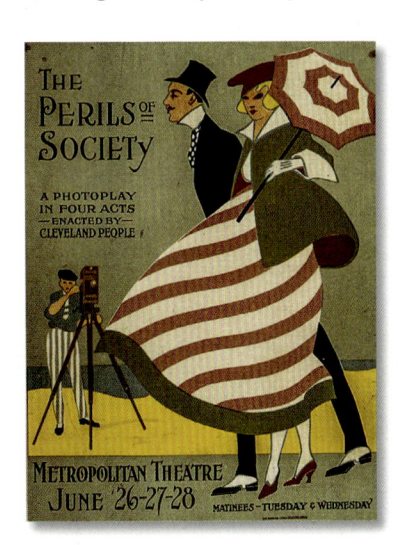

Exuding the elegance of the day, this poster promoted the benefit screening of *Perils of Society* in 1916.

During the filming of *Fast 8*, the latest in the *Fast and Furious* series, filmed on the streets of Cleveland.

CLEVELAND A to Z

ANNA PERKINS (CA. 1849–1900)

Scan to learn more

Challenging gendered boundaries is, at times, problematic today. During the late nineteenth century, it was even more problematic. But Anna Perkins, usually referred to as "Newspaper Annie," did just that.

Anna is often treated as a curiosity in the city's history and that is a disservice both to her and to Cleveland. She was born in Green Springs, Ohio, and brought up in Berlin Heights, Ohio, where being unconventional was the norm. It had been home to what some might term today a commune, where free love, radical dress, and nude bathing challenged Victorian values. There, Anna turned to poetry, her own version of vegetarianism, a belief in alternative medicines, and fashion reform—she wore trousers, a men's jacket, and cropped her hair.

Her life story is complex. Sources indicate that she treated her parents badly—her beliefs in medicine and lifestyle were not theirs. On her own after their deaths, she became, according to local memory, the town outcast, living simply and roughly, but adhering to her own tenets. She promoted those beliefs, particularly dress reform, in poetry that she published. Two stanzas read as follows:

> Yes, I know you think
> it queer,
> Well for him, then well
> for her
> That in this attire
> I appear;
> Nature's sex doth not
> prefer
> But this suit is good
> and grand—
> Leaves me free in foot
> and hand.

In 1887 she came to Cleveland where she took a job as a "newsboy" selling the *Cleveland Press* at two cents a copy on Public Square—making a penny on each copy sold. The sight of a thirty-eight-year-old woman, dressed in men's clothing and competing with young newsies roused both curiosity and ire, but eventually the community accepted her. In Cleveland her commitment to challenging the norm was proven not only in her costume and in her sparse living arrangement in a series of rundown apartment rooms, but also by her attendance at liberal discussion forums, such as the Franklin Club and the women's Sorosis.

She died in February 1900 of typhoid. Cared for at St. Alexis Hospital, she refused medication and any food that contained meat or vegetables (she had subsisted on raw fruit, crackers, and water). The president of the Franklin Club noted her passing by saying, "As a society seeking social progress in all directions, we cannot help to admire the steadfastness with which she stood by in her convictions as a social reformer."

Anna went home to Berlin Heights where she is buried beside her parents. One of her costumes is preserved at the Western Reserve Historical Society.

Anna Perkins, dressed to her own style and taste, sells copies of the *Cleveland Press* on Public Square on March 10, 1892.

Newspaper Annie's outfit, matched with a period hat, in the Costume and Textile Collection of the Western Reserve Historical Society.

PIEROGIES

Scan to learn more

There are three Ps that define Cleveland as a city with a strong eastern and central European heritage: pierogies, Parma, and polka. Pierogies are not haute cuisine but rather a Slavic soul food, if you will. Take unleavened dough, fill it with cheese, sauerkraut, potatoes, or meat (if you can afford it and if it's not Lent); crimp the edges; boil the dumpling; and then bake or fry it. To enhance the taste, fry the pierogi in lots of butter with onions. It's cheap, simple, and very filling—and great with a cold beer after a long day at the factory.

Today pierogies have gone a bit upscale (not unlike other basic ethnic foods, such as polenta) and are ubiquitous in Cleveland. You can find them frozen or fresh in many supermarkets, even at some of the more upscale ones. But the best ones still have a real connection to the community. Check out any Eastern or central European church festival in Cleveland. Chances are that the ladies of the church will have made fresh pierogies to be sold as fund-raisers.

Even though linked specifically to Poles, Ukrainians, and other Slavic groups, pierogies can also be seen as a universal symbol of ethnicity in Greater Cleveland and the communalities of food that often bind people of diverse backgrounds together. Dough, leavened or unleavened, and then filled with everything from fruits to meats can be found in the cuisines of many of the 100 plus ethnicities in the region. Think of Asian Indian samosas, Cornish pasties, Jewish kreplach, Mexican empanadas, Italian ravioli and tortellini, Turkish borek, and Arab fatayar. Given the shifts in immigration patterns in the recent past, future Clevelanders may soon elevate another basic ethnic food to the level of the pierogi as a culinary symbol of the city and its people.

Only in Cleveland could one find a song devoted to the pierogi on a record with a jacket containing the images of local media heroes, such as Ghoulardi and Dick Goddard.

Making pierogies in the kitchen of Seven Roses, a Polish restaurant in Cleveland's Slavic Village.

CLEVELAND A to Z

PITTSBURGH

Yes, Cleveland's archrival city, Pittsburgh, deserves its own entry in a guide to the city. A review of the relationship between the two cities can add much to understanding Cleveland's psyche.

In 1799, only three years after Cleveland was founded, it was connected by road to Pittsburgh. That road was initially known as (you guessed it) the Pittsburgh Road. Today that road endures and is known as Broadway, part of State Route 14 that runs to the Pennsylvania border, becomes Route 51, and ends in Pittsburgh. In the mid-1850s, Cleveland gained a second connection to Pittsburgh, a railroad, one of the first major lines to be built from the city.

Commerce between the two cities was important, particularly as each grew in the mid-nineteenth century. But as the cities industrialized, the relationship became more competitive. Cleveland's Board of Trade (later to become the Chamber of Commerce) was always concerned about keeping up with Pittsburgh, particularly in heavy industries such as iron and steel. It argued against proposed air pollution regulations because they might give Pittsburgh the advantage. By the late nineteenth century, a pall of air pollution in both cities testified to a vigorous competition that would endure until after World War II.

At that point, the game shifted. Pittsburgh realized that steel would no longer be its dominant industry and that pollution was an enemy to its image and to the health of its citizens. Its first renaissance project accomplished that goal. Cleveland would follow with its own environmental triage, inspired by Pittsburgh, but driven by new federal regulations. Pittsburgh's second renaissance project, which focused on creating a solid postindustrial economic plan also served to inspire (perhaps goad) Cleveland. The "what's Pittsburgh doing?" question remains common in Cleveland today.

Economics, however, take a backseat to the biggest rivalry between the two cities—football. That rivalry is a reminder of their shared blue-collar industrial background. American pro football is a sport that first took hold in the industrial cities of the Midwest. Rougher and less refined than the collegiate version, it appealed to the immigrant and migrant workers and their children who labored in the mills and factories. Chicago Bears coach Mike Ditka hit the mark about the nature of pro ball when he characterized his Bears as a Grabowski rather than a Smith team—certain surnames tend to exude a working-class aura.

The Browns–Steelers rivalry is where the cities truly clash in what has become known as the Turnpike War and is on a par with the collegiate Ohio State–Michigan rivalry. In both instances the full season record doesn't matter "that much" so long as the season includes a victory over one's nemesis. And, that turnpike connection allows fans to easily follow their favorite team into the enemy's stadium.

The Browns and Steelers first met in 1950, just after the Browns had joined the NFL after a spectacular career in the All-American Football Conference. It was a time when the mills were still smoking and the seats still affordable. From 1950 to 1970, the Browns won 31 of 40 regular season games. Then the tables turned. Since the 1970s (through 2018), the Steelers have been dominant, winning 66 of 98 contests. The fact that the Steelers now are ahead in the overall contest does not sit well with Cleveland fans. But as Cleveland sports fans have come to learn—there's always next year!

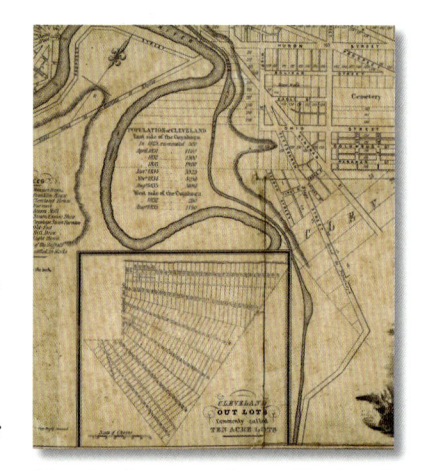

The one-time Pittsburgh Road first traces the east side of the Flats and then cuts south to face the steel mills in the Flats head on.

Cleveland's connection to Pittsburgh started just to the southeast of Public Square in 1835 on a street named, of course, Pittsburgh.

POLKA

Scan to learn more

The sign in front of this polka band playing ca. 1945 says a great deal about Cleveland's musical culture at that time. The polka "king" Frankie Yankovic stands fifth from left. National Cleveland-Style Polka Hall of Fame.

Cleveland has two music halls of fame, the Rock Hall and the National Cleveland-Style Polka Hall of Fame. The former is well known, the latter, located in Euclid, Ohio, is not on everyone's radar, but some would argue that it is a better exemplar of the area's musical tastes and contributions than the Rock Hall. That debate aside, the Polka Hall of Fame has much to say about what Cleveland was in regard to popular culture at a particular point in time, a time when many residents or their parents had come from Europe. The music at festivals, weddings, on the street, and on the radio focused on the immigrant audience and their homeland, or it was quite often a hybrid of European and American styles. The polka was predominant, leveraged on the accordion and played in a variety of styles that reflected particular immigrant group tastes and styles. Those who loved polka had their preferences—a slower Slovenian ballroom style, the Polish style dominated by wind instruments, or a brassy German style. Although polka was a common format in many industrial immigrant cities in the twentieth century, Cleveland was acknowledged as "America's Polka Capital." The style peaked in the years just after World War II, attracting audiences in and outside of ethnic communities. Frankie Yankovic who grew up in the Collinwood Slovenian community was central to that growth. Two of his post–World War II recordings sold millions in an era when that level of sale was truly high. But within two decades, the interest in polka had waned, a decline driven by the rising popularity of rock and roll and the aging of the older generations.

Yet polka persists, both in its older forms and in new fusions with styles such as country and western. It is a background sound for the region's history along with the blues, rock and roll, salsa, and mariachi. Find the right street festival, restaurant, or wedding, and you are likely to hear a mixture of all of the above, and, if you really want to focus on polka, take a trip to Euclid, Ohio, and visit the "other" hall of fame—admission is free and the history comes with a lively musical background. Or if you want the "full" experience, go to the three-day Thanksgiving Polka Weekend sponsored by the hall of fame. Held downtown, it's known as the Woodstock of Cleveland-style polka.

A display at the National Cleveland-Style Polka Hall of Fame celebrates "America's Polka King," accordionist Frankie Yankovic.

CLEVELAND A to Z

PUBLIC SQUARE

While certainly not as large as New York's Central Park or Chicago's Millennium Park, Cleveland's oldest central urban green space is far more representative of the city's origins than these more famous urban open spaces. It is truly a town commons, a concept familiar and dear to the city's New England founders. It is central to the first town plan/map of Cleveland drawn by Amos Spafford in 1796. As the city began to grow in the 1820s and 1830s, the Square acquired the usual accoutrements of a New England commons around its periphery—a church, a courthouse, a hotel or inn, and small businesses.

As the city grew from village to metropolis in the years after 1850, this prime piece of urban real estate became a site of contention. The Fence War of 1857 was a legal battle over a fence that had been built around the entire square in order to preserve its unity as a park. Business interests wanted the intersecting streets (Ontario and Superior) open for traffic. The proponents of the enclosure won, but by 1867 the fence was history. Other debates surrounded the placement of monuments on the Square and, at one point, a plan to build a grandiose city hall on it.

Despite the press of commerce and profit, the Square survived. Other New England–style commons in northeastern Ohio have been partially lost to progress. Today, Public Square is one of Cleveland's principal urban amenities. In 2016 it was fully redesigned and renovated, becoming greener and more park-like, and, in an echo of the Fence War, substantially restricted to vehicular traffic. Though transformed, the Square is still a reminder of the community's cultural origins, enhanced by the fact that a church, a courthouse, a hotel, and other businesses (including a casino) mark its periphery.

The Grand Opening Ceremony of the transformed Public Square took place in time for the Republican National Convention.

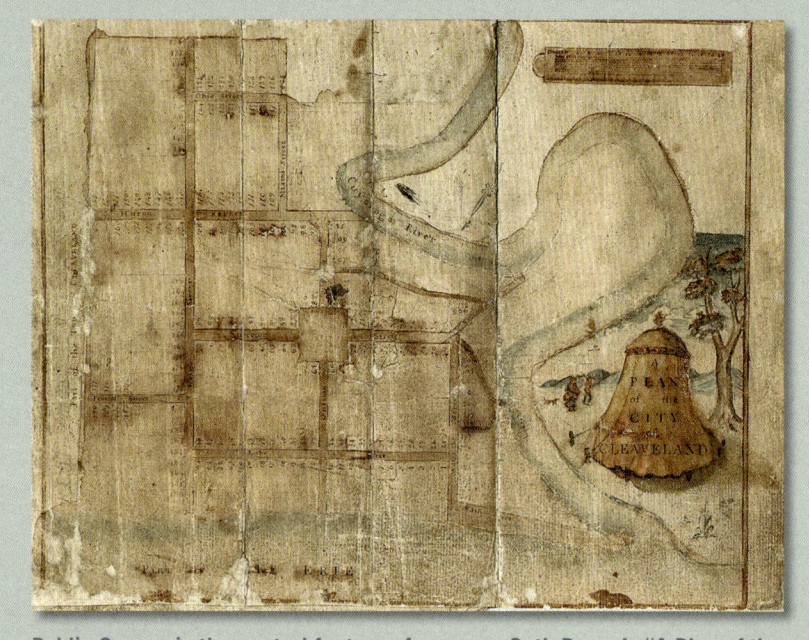

Public Square is the central feature of surveyor Seth Pease's "A Plan of the City of Cleaveland" drawing in 1796.

THOMAS QUAYLE (1811–1895)

Scan to learn more

A ship sits ready for launch on the slipway of the Cleveland Shipbuilding Company, ca. 1890.

Thomas Quayle may seem to be included in this book because his name begins with Q. That is true, but Mr. Quayle, who is not the subject of any substantial memorial, is important because of where he came from and what he did in nineteenth-century Cleveland.

Quayle was an immigrant from the Isle of Man. He was part of a substantial migration from the Isle of Man to Cleveland, so large that Cleveland is recognized as the center of Manx immigration to United States. While many in Cleveland are unaware of this fact, the Isle of Man has not forgotten. Indeed, in 1975 it issued a series of stamps that commemorated Manx immigrants to northeastern Ohio. This, however, is more than an interesting bit of "migration trivia" (something that ethnic Clevelanders engage in with gusto). It is a reminder that many of the early settlers in the region had links, either direct or through family lineage, to Great Britain. These immigrants, often "invisible" because they spoke the language of the land (albeit in a variety of accents and brogues), helped shape the foundational culture of the community.

While many of the Manx were farmers, Quayle was a ship's carpenter, and Cleveland was a center for shipbuilding, an aspect of its history now absent (in large scale) from its wharves and docks. Quayle partnered with several individuals in his career and at one point his company was so busy that it turned business away. While Quayle and Sons was important, other firms were larger. The most important (chartered in New Jersey in 1899) was American Ship Building, created by the consolidation of three firms in Cleveland and five others around the Great Lakes. In 1952 it was the largest shipbuilder on the Great Lakes. Perhaps of more consequence was the fact that one of its CEOs, George Steinbrenner III, became famous as the owner of the New York Yankees, a baseball team that Clevelanders (like those in many other cities) have taken delight in despising.

While attending an Indians versus Yankees game might be an enjoyable but somewhat oblique way of remembering Mr. Quayle, a visit to Toledo's National Museum of the Great Lakes or the *William G. Mather* at the Cleveland's Great Lakes Science Center could be more appropriate—and absent the fear of a potential Yankee victory.

Ship building is alive and well in Cleveland. This tugboat is under construction at Great Lakes Shipyard.

CLEVELAND A to Z

JOHN D. ROCKEFELLER (1839–1937)

John D. Rockefeller is arguably the wealthiest and most famous individual to have lived in Cleveland. It was the city in which he received his business education and in which he began Standard Oil. Yet he eventually left the city. Some contend that he was driven away, and had that not been the case then, perhaps, Cleveland, and not New York, would be the site of something akin to Rockefeller Center.

Rich, handsome, and in his forties, John D. Rockefeller posed for this image in a New York studio in the 1880s.

That Rockefeller left Cleveland is indisputable, but his ties to the city remained strong. He originally came to the area, settling in Strongsville, with members of his family in 1853. He attended Central High School and a local business college and by 1855 was working for a commission house in the Flats. By 1859 he was in partnership in a commission business that prospered by selling grains and other commodities during the Civil War. In 1863 he began dealing with petroleum and seven years later established Standard Oil. By 1880 he was worth $18 million, a considerable sum for the time. Four years later he bought a home in New York, attracted to the city not by its urbanity and culture, but by the capital available in its banks and investment houses—because by the 1880s Rockefeller had tapped out most of the capital available in Cleveland. However, he returned each year to spend time at his estate, Forest Hill, situated in what is now Cleveland Heights and East Cleveland. He also owned a home at East 40th and Euclid, which he used infrequently.

His affinity for the city may well have ended in 1913–1914. During that period he extended his usual summer stay at Forest Hill because his wife, Cettie, had become seriously ill and could not be transported back to New York. Eventually, they returned. However, Cuyahoga County officials argued that the extended stay made Rockefeller eligible for a tax payment. They claimed he owed the county $2.25 million. He fought the assessment and stayed out of Cleveland for fear of subpoena. The case was still active when Cettie died in March 1915 and prevented the family's return to Cleveland for her burial at Lake View Cemetery until the assessment was dropped five months later. It was not a pleasant experience for Rockefeller or for his son, John D. Jr.

Nevertheless, the connection to Cleveland continued. His son developed part of Forest Hill for housing, funds continued to come to support his church, Euclid Avenue Baptist, as well as Alta Social Settlement (named after his daughter, Alta Rockefeller Prentiss) in Little Italy. In 1937 Rockefeller died at his Florida home and his body was transported to Cleveland for burial at the family plot in Lake View. That plot along with Rockefeller Park, the Rockefeller Building on Superior at West 6th, and the Rockefeller Physics Building at CWRU are tangible reminders of his connection to Cleveland. They may not equal Rockefeller Center in size, but they evidence his local entrepreneurial roots and his considerable charitable gifts to the city. They add up to much more than the dimes he became famous for handing out to friends and strangers on the street. Today, when visiting the family plot at Lake View, many people leave a dime or two on his tombstone.

Known for giving dimes to strangers, the visitors to Rockefeller's grave leave dimes in return.

Goulder, Grace. *John D. Rockefeller: The Cleveland Years*. Cleveland: Western Reserve Historical Society, 1973.

SHAKER HEIGHTS

Scan to learn more

The simple structures of the North Union Shaker Community shown in this ca. 1870s photograph would present a stark contrast to the structures in today's Shaker Heights.

Of all the "Heights" suburbs surrounding Cleveland, Shaker Heights is one of the wealthiest and historically significant. Indeed, it is featured in *Crabgrass Frontier* by Kenneth T. Jackson, one of the best books ever written on American suburbanization.

Created by the two Van Sweringen brothers in the first decade of the twentieth century, Shaker is a nationally significant model of suburban planning. Its curved streets and parks are a hallmark of the town, as are its carefully planned set of sub-communities, defined by housing and lot size and consequently by income and status. While envisioned as a white upper-class sanctuary away from the city, Shaker also gained fame in the 1960s and 1970s when it successfully integrated largely though grassroots efforts organized by the Ludlow and Lomond associations within the community.

While the story of the creation and transition of Shaker is significant, its earliest history leads to something arguably more interesting—the history of nontraditional religion and belief in northeastern Ohio. Shaker is built on land that was once one of the nineteen major communities in the United States created by the United Society of Believers in Christ's Second Appearing, a sect founded by Ann Lee in England in the eighteenth century. The Shaking Quakers, or "Shakers," were one of the many religious and communal experiments that took root in the United States. North Union, as the community was named, lasted from 1822 to 1889. It, like other Shaker communities, suffered because the sect's belief in celibacy made natural replenishment of the community impossible. When the remaining Shakers moved out, the land became a prime candidate for development, and the era of plain people who believed in simple gifts and eschewed extravagance was truly over. But the Shakers were not the only nontraditional religious or communal group to find a home in northeastern Ohio.

The Latter Day Saints, or Mormons, called Kirtland home from 1831 to 1838. The first temple they built still stands on Route 306. Cleveland was also home to a group of "Millerites," part of an Adventist group established by William Miller in New York in the 1830s. Twice, in 1843 and 1844, they expected the Day of Judgment and gathered in a specially constructed temple on Wood (East 3rd) Street near Rockwell waiting to rise to heaven through the opening they had left in the top of the structure. In the 1850s a group of "sex radicals" established a free-love commune in Berlin Heights, west of Cleveland. It had an on-and-off existence over the years with changes in focus and purpose, but it always challenged the tenets of society. They promoted their beliefs and lifestyles through the newspapers they published, including two titled *The Age of Freedom* and *The Good Time Coming*. Like the Van Sweringens, the dreamers at Berlin Heights wished to reshape the way we live, and that begs the question as to who had the better solution.

These gateposts, near Lee Road, are remnants of the North Union Shaker Community.

CLEVELAND A to Z

BELLE SHERWIN (1868–1955)

Scan to learn more

Belle Sherwin, local and national advocate for women's suffrage.

Certainly the name Sherwin has wide recognition in Cleveland, particularly as part of Sherwin Williams, one of the oldest corporations in the city. Yet there is another Sherwin that deserves equal public notice and not simply because she was the daughter of one of the founders of the coatings company.

Belle Sherwin epitomized the Progressive woman. Educated at Wellesley and having done graduate work at Oxford, she became a major force in social reform and particularly in the drive for women's rights. Her progressive CV, so to speak, included work with the Consumers League (an agency focused on preventing the exploitation of child laborers) which she organized in 1899, as well as the Visiting Nurse Association. In World War I she coordinated the work of local women when the city began to mobilize its resources.

All of this was important and critical to a changing city, but her key contribution was her focus on women's suffrage. She became involved in the movement in 1910 when she joined the College Equal Suffrage League. In 1919 she became president of the Women Suffrage Party of Greater Cleveland. The following year, with the passage of the Nineteenth Amendment, American women finally gained the national right to vote. But that victory was not an end point for Belle Sherwin—she became the chair of the Cleveland League for Women Voters and in 1921 the vice president of the National League of Women Voters. Three years later she became president of the national organization and moved to Washington.

Certainly Belle Sherwin was not alone in her campaign for suffrage. Others, such as Florence Ellinwood Allen, who became the first female judge on the state's supreme court, and Elizabeth Hauser, a newspaper reporter, were, with hundreds of other women, active in the causes of suffrage and progressive reform in the city and the nation. Indeed, if one looks deeper into the city and the nation's history, the role of women in a variety of reform causes, such as abolition and antislavery, was considerable and highly effective. Sherwin and her sister reformers

This period display at the Cleveland History Center is a tribute to the role of progressive women in northeast Ohio.

effectively helped create the city and world we live in today. One wonders what they might think of a major party female candidate for president running for office only four years before the anniversary of the Nineteenth Amendment.

THE SHOREWAY

Scan to learn more

Every evening thousands of eastbound commuters exit downtown via the "Innerbelt," negotiate "Dead Man's Curve," and then head east on Interstate 90. In doing so, they are traversing both excavation and fill, as well as some fine points of local nomenclature.

The Innerbelt is an excavated gash through downtown Cleveland designed to connect Interstate 77 and 71 with Interstate 90. Its construction in the late 1950s and early 1960s did much to alter the central urban landscape of the city. When it was cut through Euclid Avenue, for example, it took out the Leonard Hanna Mansion, the only structure on Cleveland's Millionaires' Row that was designed by the renowned New York architect, Stanford White. It just missed the Samuel Mather Mansion to the west, which, fortunately, remains one of few along Euclid that stands fully intact.

Once someone enters I-90 going east, the encounter is equally historic. This is the Shoreway, constructed in the late 1930s as one of the first parts of a system of limited access roads that would serve Cleveland. Planners felt they would make life in the city more attractive by taking heavy traffic off of city streets. Ultimately the arteries they envisioned would serve largely as a convenient exit from the city to new homes in the suburbs.

The project was undertaken by the WPA and thus supported in large part by federal funds. While the Innerbelt was constructed in a cut, this section of the Shoreway was built on a landfill that extended the shoreline of the city into the lake. The original lakeshore rises just south of the highway. It houses another transport artery: the main east-west rail line through Cleveland, which was initially built in the 1850s.

After World War II the road was widened and improved and renamed the Memorial Shoreway to honor veterans. A western extension carried it through Edgewater Park to Clifton Boulevard and thus provided the city with another east-west dichotomy—the West Shoreway and the East Shoreway. Eventually the eastern section was joined with the Lakeland Freeway and both became part of Interstate 90, the federal highway system begun in 1956.

This 1930s aerial photograph of the area near East 55th shows landfill creeping into Lake Erie. That process would eventually make possible not only the Shoreway but a stadium and an airport.

Approaching downtown on the Shoreway from the east, drivers are faced with a choice of continuing to Lakewood or through "Dead Man's Curve" to I-71, I-77, and I-90.

CLEVELAND A to Z

SHORT VINCENT STREET

Scan to learn more

A Cleveland policeman walks what might have been the city's most interesting beat in 1964—the bars and nightclubs of Short Vincent. Special Collections, Michael Schwartz Library, Cleveland State University.

With a Short Vincent Street in Cleveland, one might expect there to be a "Long Vincent" Street too. There is neither, but there is a Vincent Street that runs from East Ninth to East Sixth Street just north of Euclid Avenue. To a dwindling number of older Clevelanders, this was Short Vincent and to them it was the street where one could get the odds on anything, with the lure of sex and sin just around the corner.

In its heyday, which lasted from the 1930s to the late 1950s, Short Vincent was lined with bars and eateries, which attracted gamblers, mobsters, sports figures, and many journalists. It was an all-night venue located just around the corner from the Roxy Burlesque Theater and Jean's Fun House, an arcade filled with games and peep shows. It is tempting to say that Short Vincent was Cleveland's version of Las Vegas, but that would be understating its importance.

Some of the entrepreneurs and habitués of the area, known as the "Gaza Strip," were among the founders of Sin City, which rose to prominence in the 1950s and 1960s. While Vegas rose, Short Vincent gave way to urban renewal when major banking complexes rose on both sides of the street in the 1960s and 1970s.

The best way to experience this Cleveland classic is to read James Neff's *Mobbed Up* and James Wood's *Out and About with Winsor French*. Or you could try a trip to Vegas where a trip to the Mob Museum will clearly outline Cleveland's connection to that city.

Today, structural changes along the street make it difficult to imagine the rich history of Short Vincent.

CLEVELAND A to Z

SLAVIC VILLAGE

Scan to learn more

Old-world architecture and new development combine to bring back neighborhoods that were hard-hit during the sub-prime mortgage crisis.

If you exit Interstate 77 at Fleet Avenue and drive east toward Broadway, look closely and you will discern carved wooden decorative elements on some of the buildings. They are there to tell you that you are in Slavic Village, one of the city's many neighborhoods. However, the Tatra Mountain Hylander décor is not original to the area. It dates from the late 1970s when neighborhood leaders sought to rebrand the neighborhood and, perhaps, make it an attraction as viable as Little Italy.

The identity switch for Slavic Village involved more than the application of a new architectural look. It also subsumed the original identities of the area. The western end of Fleet Avenue was known as Karlin, which is a suburb of Prague (Praha) in the Czech Republic. Its residents were, in large part, Czech. The eastern end was known as Warszawa (Warsaw), the capital of Poland. Its residents were Polish and like the Czechs, Slavs. So the rebranding made ethnological sense, despite protests from some residents.

Today Slavic Village fills much of South/North Broadway constituting two of the formal planning districts in the city—which serve, in a sense, to obscure a multitude of organic identities: Warszawa and Karlin are now sharing space with Jackowa (St. Hyacinth), Krakowa (Krakow), and Praha (Prague), all names that still have resonance to older Clevelanders and all part of the rich panoply of identity in a city of nineteenth- and early twentieth-century ethnic villages where most had their own name. Dutch Hill, Buckeye, Duck Island, Little Italy, Big Italy, Cedar-Central, the Angle, and Glenville are still there as are their histories—a multitude of micro-stories that constitute the history of the city and region over the past 230 years. And that post-settlement history begs the question as to what names the area's original Native American settlers gave to the landscapes that they inhabited. What, to close the story of Slavic Village, did they call the burial mound (after which Mound Avenue is named), which stood on the bluff of Morgan Run, the creek that one day would come to demark the boundary between Czech Praha and Polish Warszawa?

A reproduction of a rare 1880s lithograph shows St. Stanislaus Church and school in what was then called Warszawa, the city's primary Polish neighborhood.

CLEVELAND A to Z

SOM CENTER ROAD

Brick by brick, laborers create a new pavement for SOM Center Road in 1916.

SOM Center Road is one of the major non-freeway arteries on Cleveland's East Side. Running north and south, it is an outer-ring suburb commuting route. It constitutes a portion of State Route 91 and received its current name in the 1920s. Crowded at times, particularly near its intersection with Mayfield, it can sometimes be a vexing drive. However, it is an even more vexing test of one's knowledge of local pronunciation. Does one pronounce SOM as a single word or as a series of single letters? Use of the latter pronunciation marks one as a local greenhorn. But not to worry—you're not alone, for not many people really know the origin of the name. And if they think they do, they often only come close to the truth.

The route is the Solon, Orange, and Mayfield Road, and it is so named not because of the two villages (Orange and Mayfield) and one city (Solon) situated on it today but because of the townships that the road has connected since the nineteenth century. Those townships, and all other townships in the Western Reserve, have an interesting story to tell. They are creations of the early surveys of the Reserve conducted in 1796 and 1797. They are square plots set upon a natural landscape—truly human creations typical of the ideals of the Enlightenment and foundational to the creation of the United States. They carry out a concept expressed in one of the early formative pieces of national legislation, the Ordinance of 1785, which set the standards for the way the nation's lands west of the Appalachians would be surveyed and divided for sale. The land was to be divided into square townships measuring six miles on each side. But plans went slightly differently in the survey of the Western Reserve where townships measure five miles per side. This "rational" peculiarity sets northeastern Ohio apart from other parts of the former Northwest Territory, and it also makes one's township-to-township drive along SOM Center Road slightly shorter than a similar drive outside the Western Reserve.

The intersection of SOM Center and Wilson Mills Roads, in what once was Mayfield Center.

60 CLEVELAND A to Z

STOKES

Carl and Louis Stokes pose with their mother Louise, whose determination and hard work underlay their success.

If you are a careful observer of the names of buildings, streets, and civic landmarks in Cleveland, you will notice how often the name "Stokes" appears. There is Stokes Boulevard in University Circle, the Stokes Rapid Transit station in East Cleveland, and a Stokes building at the School of Medicine at Case Western Reserve University. The name also appears on a wing of the Cleveland Public Library, on the VA Hospital at University Circle, and on the federal courthouse. All recognize and honor either Carl (1927–1996) or Louis Stokes (1925–2015), brothers who helped reshape American politics in the last third of the twentieth century. Carl, elected mayor of Cleveland in 1967, was the first African American mayor of a major American city, while Louis was a fifteen-term (1969–1999) member of the House of Representatives where, among other leadership roles, he chaired the House Select Committee on Assassinations.

Their achievements represent one of the city's most remarkable Horatio Alger stories. Their parents, Charles and Louise Stokes, were part of the Great Migration of African Americans from the South to northern cities like Cleveland, arriving in the 1920s. Three years after Carl's birth, his father, a laundryman, died, leaving his mother, a cleaning woman, to raise the two boys. They grew up in Outhwaite Homes, the city's first federally funded housing project and a place that Carl remembered as a remarkable step up from where they had previously lived. Inspired and encouraged by their mother, both eventually worked their way through college and law school and then went into politics. Carl's election as mayor was national news, and he made the cover of *Time* magazine. Lou, as head of the Select Committee on Assassinations, would come face to face with James Earl Ray, the killer of Dr. Martin Luther King Jr.; he would later confront Col. Oliver North during the hearings on the Iran-Contra scandal in the 1980s. Both were central figures, albeit working in different styles, in the Civil Rights movement of the 1960s and the decades thereafter.

The political success of the Stokes brothers in Cleveland during the 1960s is one of the indicators of the potential the community had, and still retains, in regard to race. Carl was elected when the majority of the electorate was white.

Two decades earlier, the Cleveland Indians made Larry Doby the first African American player in the American League, and one year before that, the Cleveland Browns, by hiring Marion Motley and Bill Willis in 1946, helped integrate professional football. While symbols such as these do not necessarily reflect a broader reality, they are powerful reminders of an ability to change. The signs that read "Stokes" help keep that lesson in mind.

Moore, Leonard N. *Carl B. Stokes and the Rise of Black Political Power.* Urbana: Univ. of Illinois Press, 2002.

Stradling, David, and Richard Stradling. *Where the River Burned: Carl Stokes and the Struggle to Save Cleveland.* Ithaca: Cornell Univ. Press, 2015.

The childhood home of the Stokes brothers stands in what was one of the city's first federally funded housing projects.

TIME MAGAZINE

Scan to learn more

For two years in the mid-1920s, the issues of *Time* magazine were printed in the Penton Building at West 3rd and Lakeside.

Looking toward the Flats from the window of the studio of photographer Margaret Bourke-White in the Terminal Tower.

During the Gatsby era, Cleveland was home to one of America's premiere weekly news magazines. It was only for a two-year period, from 1925 to 1927, but the move of *Time* to Cleveland reflected upon some important aspects of the city during the Roaring Twenties. One was the centrality of the city to national markets during an era when most mail and goods moved by rail. *Time* had started out in New York City in 1923, but the publishers soon found the East Coast location made a prompt arrival of the magazine on the West Coast problematic. Then, too, Cleveland was one of the centers of commercial publishing with a huge variety of printing and design firms, including Penton Publishing, which handled the account. It was during the two-year tenure in Cleveland that *Time* acquired its classic red cover border.

While Clevelanders could take delight in Gotham's loss, one of the editors, Britton Haddon, found the city not up to his cosmopolitan tastes, nor a good site for quick access to major national and international news. Indeed, his partner, Henry Luce, had engineered the move out of New York when Britton was away in Europe. When Luce went to Europe two years later, Britton moved the operation back to New York! Nevertheless, *Time*'s sojourn in Cleveland would have residual effects on national journalism. When Luce revived *Life* magazine as a pictorial in 1936, his first issue contained stunning images by Margaret Bourke-White, whose work Luce had become acquainted with during his time in Cleveland and which he then later incorporated in another of his magazines, *Fortune*.

UNIVERSITY CIRCLE

Scan to learn more

University Circle, Cleveland, Ohio.

The namesakes of University Circle—the main buildings of the Case School of Applied Sciences and Western Reserve University and the traffic circle on Euclid Avenue—dominate the view in this early 1900s postcard.

Cleveland's Acropolis is University Circle, home to parks, museums, music, hospitals, and, of course, a university. There are many aspects of the Circle that are interesting, but perhaps most interesting is its origin story—both in terms of place and name.

It is located at its present site because of Doan Brook, which, as noted earlier in this volume, not only anchored an early settlement, but created a landscape that would be central to the ultimate creation of University Circle. The major question is how did the landscape get renamed in academic and geometric terms?

The university part of the name (or, more properly, universities) came first. Western Reserve College, established in 1826, was the first institution of higher education in northeastern Ohio. It was founded in Hudson at a time when that village and Cleveland were roughly equivalent in size. Cleveland, however, grew while Hudson stayed rural. By mid-century it seemed logical to some that Cleveland might be the better location for the college. But there were concerns. Cleveland was a lake port, complete with all the vices one might find among sailors, vices that might well transfer to the student body. The debate and discussion ended in 1882 when a gift of $500,000 from railroad builder Amasa Stone brought the college to Cleveland on a campus then far distant from the vices of the city. Both the gift and location were keys to the decision. Additional money was raised for purchase of the campus with the understanding that another institution, the Case School of Applied Sciences (founded in 1880 and initially located in the city) would move five miles east and construct its campus adjacent to that of Western Reserve. The two institutions began cooperatively but then existed adjacent and separately and, at times, competitively. The athletic contests between the schools were intense—the annual Case vs. Western Reserve football game was a highlight of the local sporting calendar. Although the schools merged in 1967, forming Case Western Reserve University, the athletic competition, because of preset conference schedules, continued for several additional years—highlighted by students bearing signs inscribed, "If we lose, we win" or "If we win, we lose." The term "Circle" was applied to the area at the turn of the twentieth century when a traffic circle was constructed on Euclid Avenue just east of what today is Stokes Boulevard. A streetcar line ran east-west through the center of the circle where a branch switched south along Stearns Road.

Today it's relatively easy to find the "University" part of the name. Case Western Reserve (with a single set of athletic teams) is ranked among the top forty universities in the nation. Finding the Circle, however, is a bit problematic. One quadrant remains in front of the One University Circle building (under construction in 2017) on the south side of Euclid, and plantings outline the remaining three quadrants at the intersection of Euclid Avenue and Stearns Road.

Sponsored by the Cleveland Museum of Art, the annual Parade the Circle has brought cultural and community organizations together in University Circle since 1990.

CLEVELAND A to Z

THE "VANS"

When a Clevelander speaks of "the Vans," the immediate assumption is that someone is moving or the Indians are off to spring training. Chances are, however, that she or he is referring to the Van Sweringen brothers who were responsible for creating Cleveland's iconic Terminal Tower and one of its premier suburbs, Shaker Heights.

The Vans—O. P. (Oris Paxton) and M. J. (Mantis James)—were bachelor brothers who built a real estate and railroad empire in northeastern Ohio from 1910 to 1930. Theirs is an interesting and complex story. As the city's population expanded by over 400,000 in the three decades between 1890 and 1920, real estate evolved into a major industry with fortunes waiting to be made. The brothers began their venture (unsuccessfully) in the new suburb of Lakewood. They then went east of the river where they created Shaker Heights. But their arc of entrepreneurship expanded beyond property. The simplification of a complex story is as follows. To make Shaker Heights successful, they needed light rail access to the city center. So they built an interurban (today's RTA Blue and Green Lines). To get the interurban to the city center, they needed to use an existing railroad right-of-way. So they bought the railroad and then another and another. Then they needed a terminal in the city. Initially envisioned as a small interurban terminal, it eventually morphed into the Cleveland Union Terminal complex comprised of several major buildings and a fifty-two-story tower that would remain the tallest structure outside of New York City until the 1960s. Its construction, along with the requisite rail lines, was an enormous project that garnered national attention. It was Cleveland's Rockefeller Center (albeit, completed before the center).

The Vans' empire, built on a financial pyramid that rested on stock values, would collapse during the Great Depression. M. J. died in 1935 and O. P. in 1936. Despite the enormity of their accomplishment, the brothers remain a historical cypher. During an era of Gatsbyesque extravagance, they eschewed publicity—for example, they chose not to attend the grand dedication of the Terminal in 1930.

You can find them today buried in Lake View Cemetery—their monument is of respectable size and keeping with their personal desires. However, their true monument is the change they made on the landscape of the community, a change that makes everyone curious as to who the "Vans" were.

Harwood, Herbert H. *Invisible Giants: The Empires of Cleveland's Van Sweringen Brothers.* Bloomington: Indiana Univ. Press, 2003.

It is rare to find a candid image such as this of the two Van Sweringen brothers, who seem to be on a mission of some import in the late 1920s.

The Board Room in the Van Sweringens' Greenbriar Suite on the 13th and 14th floors of the Terminal Tower.

VINEGAR HILL

Scan to learn more

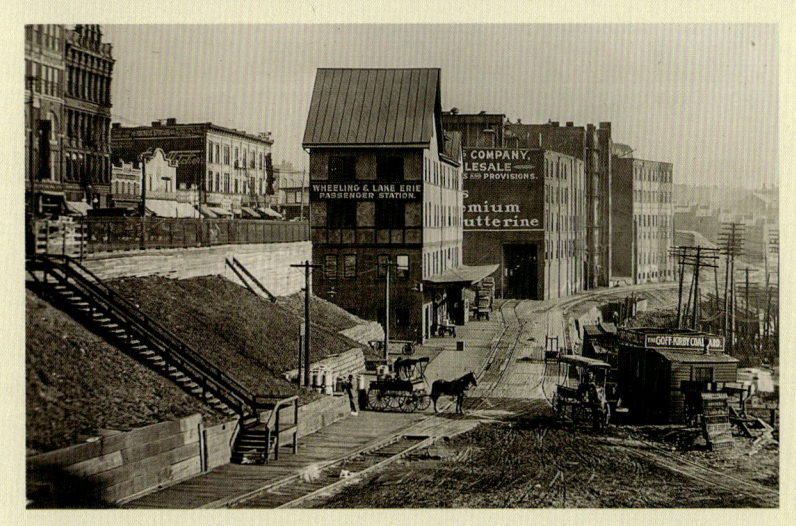

The hillside depot of the Wheeling and Lake Erie Terminal overlooks the region in the Flats known as Vinegar Hill in 1914. The depot would be demolished for construction of the Union Terminal complex.

Among Cleveland's forgotten landmarks is a site once referred to as Vinegar Hill. It referred to the bluff off the hillside (today just south of Tower City Center) that leads down to Canal Road. Its name was both current and pungent in the late nineteenth and early twentieth century when that area was a chaotic mixture of aging houses, small factories, railroad lines, and atmospheric pollutants. One of the small factories, near what are now Broadway and Carnegie, produced vinegar, the smell of which probably gave the area its name. All of this disappeared when the Terminal Tower was built—the region became part of the railroad approach to the Terminal, one that Rapid Transit commuters still traverse.

Although gone, Vinegar Hill is a reminder that at one time, a certain smell could tell you exactly where you were in Cleveland. Chemical works and a soap factory under the Harvard Denison Bridge added an unmistakable odor to that area. The repulsive smell of the stockyards indicated one was on West 65th Street near Storer Avenue. Even the millionaires on Euclid Avenue could not escape the smoke and smells that northwesterly winds brought from the lakeshore factories (which some of them owned). And even in the recent past, one knew that a trip north to Cleveland on I-77 was nearly at an end when you smelled the Republic Steel coke ovens just beyond Fleet Avenue. All of these olfactory memories are evidence of a city in its industrial heyday—a heyday that occurred absent environmental controls. They also give evidence as to why many Clevelanders chose to move away from "the good old neighborhood." It certainly may have made for an easy commute to work, but residence there often came with serious environmental risks, not to mention a continual assault on one's olfactory system.

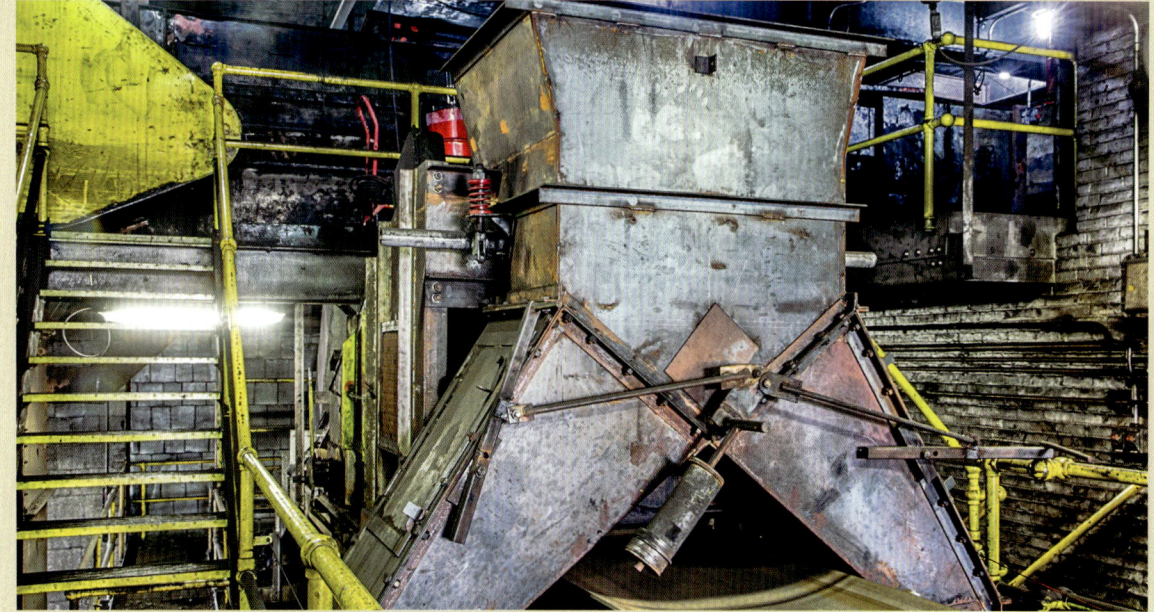

A conveyor system that delivered coal to fire the 1894 Canal Road steam plant that provided heat and steam power to the downtown commercial district.

CLEVELAND A to Z

WADE

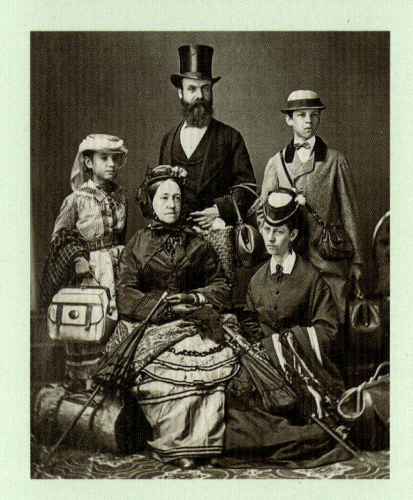

Randall Wade, son of Jeptha Homer Wade, poses with members of his family just before they embarked on a fourteen-month grand tour of Europe in 1870.

Information technology (IT) made a huge impact on Cleveland's physical and cultural landscape during the nineteenth century. That seems paradoxical given the assumption that IT has been a cultural game changer only in the last several decades. Yet it was a fortune built on what has been characterized as the "Victorian Internet" that seeded the transformation of University Circle.

Jeptha Homer Wade, a New York State native, was a portrait painter and jack-of-all-trades who became involved in the construction of early telegraph lines in the 1840s and 1850s. The invention was a marvel; it allowed the transmission of information over vast distances at a speed as fast as today's Internet. Wade was a major advocate for consolidating the early lines into larger networks. He would eventually become a founder of Western Union. The new technology made him very rich, and he relocated to Cleveland in the 1850s.

Like other wealthy Clevelanders, Wade built a house on Euclid Avenue. But he went one step further. He purchased land in the Doan Brook valley north of Euclid and created a landscaped private park, which he opened to the public in the early 1870s. In 1882 he deeded much of the park to the city. Wade Park became home to what is now the Botanical Garden, the Cleveland Museum of Natural History, and the Cleveland Museum of Art. Wade's work as a portrait painter perhaps inspired his son Randall who had a keen interest in art and museums. In 1870–1871 he and his family undertook a fourteen month trip to Europe where he viewed dozens of galleries and museums. However, his early death at age forty-one in 1876 ended any plans he may have had for similar institutions in Cleveland. His son, Jeptha "Homer" Wade II would finally catalyze the family's interest in art and culture. He was one of the primary forces behind the creation of the Cleveland Museum of Art and also a renowned collector of art and gemstones. He, his family and descendants would support the museum with significant donations of funds and works of art over the years. Today, visitors can see those collections in the art museum and in the Natural History Museum, both located on the periphery of Wade Oval, a wonderful green space situated in Wade Park in University Circle. Just across the street (East Boulevard) from the Oval, researchers and students can discover the Wades and their interests through their papers and journals preserved in the Research Library of the Western Reserve Historical Society, which is located on land once part of the Wade residential allotment.

If you wish to visit the Wades, you will find them in one of the nation's finest landscaped garden cemeteries—Lake View, which Jeptha Wade helped establish in 1869, just up the hill from his park. His monument and the graves of many members of the family are situated on a high bluff, providing a panoramic view of the landscapes he reshaped and which, in turn, reshaped Cleveland.

The final resting place of Jeptha Homer Wade and generations of his family in Lake View Cemetery.

WESTERN RESERVE/CONNECTICUT WESTERN RESERVE

The geographic definition of the Western Reserve is quite simple. Its northern boundary is Lake Erie. Its southern is north latitude 41. Its eastern boundary is the Pennsylvania state line from which it extends 120 miles to the west to the western limits of Erie and Huron Counties. Its history, however, is a deep story that intersects with global, colonial, and national events as well as an origin story of the area's cultural psyche.

What became the Western Reserve was once the home of Native Americans. The European claim to the area dates to 1662 when King Charles II confirmed a charter to the Connecticut Colony, which included all the lands situated between latitudes 40°58′ N to 42°03 and extending from "sea to sea." As the colonies grew, New York and Pennsylvania claimed lands that fell within Connecticut's grant. That contention for land then played out during the early years of independence when the colonies were asked to cede their western claims to the federal government. Because of the land it lost to Pennsylvania, Connecticut was able to "reserve" 3.3 million acres to the west in 1786. Connecticut's plan was not to settle the land, but to sell it once Native American claims were dealt with.

The legalities of this "deal" are, perhaps, a harbinger of more confusion to come. The creation of the Reserve left Connecticut in possession of lands that still belonged to Native Americans but which also had become part of the new Northwest Territory created by the Northwest Ordinance of 1787. Who really owned it? Who really was in charge? One part of this problem was settled in 1795 when native rights to the lands east of the Cuyahoga were ceded. That opened this portion of the Reserve to survey and settlement but still left the question of legal authority unresolved. The federal government assumed that Connecticut was responsible, but no one was certain. Only in 1800 with the passage of the Quieting Act did the Reserve come under the jurisdiction of the governor of the Northwest Territory.

Legalities aside, the opening, survey, and settlement of the eastern part of the Reserve in the years after 1795 marked the period when the area assumed its cultural personality. It was "New Connecticut" and more broadly, it was an outpost of New England in regard to religion, mores, and concepts of community. That set it apart from the rest of Ohio (which became a state in 1803). Predominantly Protestant, the Reserve had a moral zeal for causes such as antislavery, which were not particularly popular in the south of Ohio. That background also served as a foundation for the traditions of philanthropy and reform that grew in Cleveland. Today those echoes of the area's New England heritage complement a new reality for the Reserve. Increasingly, New Connecticut is being recreated as a rather cohesive and economically viable area called Northeastern Ohio.

Wheeler, Robert. *Visions of the Western Reserve: Public and Private Documents of Northeastern Ohio, 1750–1860*. Columbus: Ohio State Univ. Press, 2000.

This map drawn by Seth Pease in 1797 clearly shows that only that part of the Western Reserve east of the Cuyahoga River was open for settlement. Native Americans still held the rights to the land west of the river.

A replica of Lorenzo Carter's cabin, the home of Cleveland's first permanent resident.

WHISKEY ISLAND

Scan to learn more

Legends abound about the origin of the name of this small peninsula of land on the west bank of the mouth of the Cuyahoga River, many of which overestimate the quantity of spirits on the landscape, but spirits there were. The land itself is a creation of a shift in geography. It was once on the east bank of the Cuyahoga River, but the river cut another route (its current mouth) leaving the land on the west side. The old river mouth silted up and left both the peninsula and a body of stagnant water that bred hordes of mosquitoes, causing early settlers to flee the area.

One, Lorenzo Carter, stayed and started a farm on the spit of land. He eventually would move to the east bank. Later, as Irish immigrants arrived to help build the Ohio and Erie Canal and then later unload boats, they took up residence on the "Island." In the 1830s it acquired a whiskey still on the former Carter farm. That was the first hint of spirits—later it would be home to thirteen saloons, at which point its current name became common. Its isolation prompted its use as a quarantine area during an 1832 cholera epidemic. Obviously, it was not an ideal residential site, and when able, the Irish moved away.

Whiskey Island's future, as would be that for much of the city's lakefront, was to be industrial. It became part of the

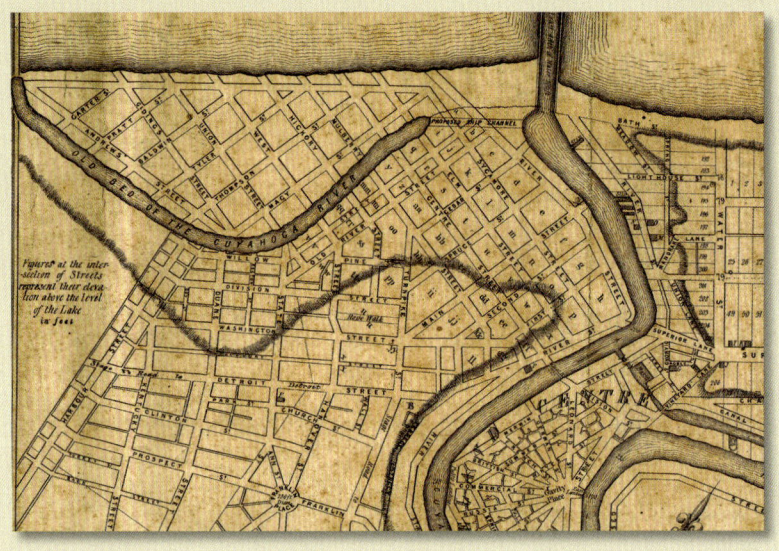

A regular street grid covered the peninsula known as Whiskey Island in 1835.

Hulett Unloaders, retired in 1998, stored on Whiskey Island, where they transferred iron ore from lake freighters to rail cars for the short trip to the steel mills.

route of the main east-west rail line through Cleveland in 1853, and that then led to a long history as an ore shipment and storage site. Part of that history—the disassembled remains of two Hulett Ore Unloaders—can be seen in storage on the Island today. It still stores ore, and it still is the entrance to a remarkable set of salt mines carved out under Lake Erie.

Today the Island is also part of a new urban recreational lifestyle—a visit provides stunning views of the city. It now houses a marina and Wendy Park, a wonderful green space on what was an industrial wasteland. Once a year Cleveland's Great Lakes Brewing Company holds its annual Burning River Fest at the old Coast Guard station just off the Island and the spirits—both in terms of heritage and drink—flow again on one of the most historic landscapes of the city.

X

It is, admittedly, hard to find aspects of Cleveland regional history that fall into the x category. The expected solution would be to choose X-ray. Certainly it fits with the city's high profile in medicine and more particularly with the Picker X-Ray Corp., which built a plant in Cleveland in 1930. Yet a scan of Cleveland's history reveals Xenophon Zapis, whose work in "ethnic media" opens up a wider historical examination of communication that is central to the city's multicultural composition.

Zapis was the founder of two "ethnic format" radio stations in Cleveland, WXEN and WZAK. During the 1960s and 1970s, they broadcast a variety of programs consisting of news and music relating to various nationality groups in the city, which at the time were predominantly central, eastern, and southern European. WZAK did so full time, WXEN part time. The format waned in the 1970s as older ethnic communities moved away, as first and second generations passed away, and as the city's demographic composition shifted—WZAK would come to focus on an African American audience.

Zapis followed in a long tradition of ethnic media in Cleveland. Cleveland's first foreign language newspaper, *Germania*, began in 1846. In the following 150 years at least 300 other titles served the informational needs and political interests of the many groups that had immigrated or migrated to the region. When radio became a popular and affordable medium, it too saw a diverse audience. Zapis followed in a path blazed by Frederick Wolf who began broadcasting a Czech language program in 1929. In 1934 he founded the Cleveland Recording Company and the Nationalities Broadcasting Association, an umbrella organization for the rapidly increasing number of ethnic programs on a wide variety of local stations.

Today, only a handful of "ethnic" newspapers remains. New sources of information for both old and new migrant groups have displaced them. Today immigrants to northeastern Ohio stay connected via satellite TV and the Internet. But there are several strong reminders of former media. WHWN (88.3 FM) and WNZN (89.2 Lorain) serve the Spanish-speaking population of the region. The *Call & Post*, established in 1927 with the merger of two older papers, remains a strong printed medium for the African American community, and WCPN, Cleveland's public radio station, devotes a portion of its weekend to ethnic programming. So if you want to tune into a multicultural tradition in Cleveland, check out 90.3 on your FM dial—German, Slovenian, Hungarian, Ukrainian, Polish, Serbian, Slovak, and Lithuanian shows are still broadcasting. Or, if AM is your band, WELW in Lake County will bring in Slovenian, Italian, Croatian, Jewish, and German music and programs with some of the best polka music on the regional airwaves.

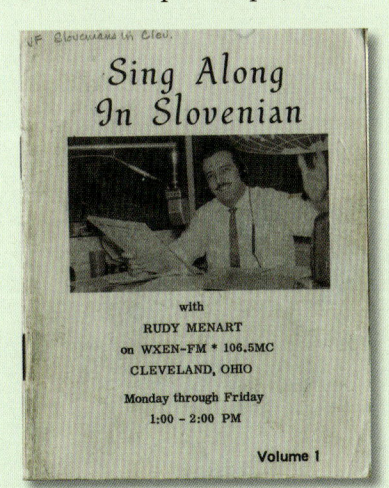

Station WXEN issued this Slovenian songbook to accompany its Slovenian language broadcasts, ca. late 1960s.

Now repurposed as an R&B station, WZAK is in its new Midtown location in a repurposed industrial building.

YELLOW CAB COMPANY

Scan to learn more

For over a half century (1934–1987), the Yellow Cab Company was the preeminent cab company in Cleveland having been granted a monopoly by the Cleveland City Council. For many of these years, cabs were numerous and highly visible in the downtown area. But perhaps more interesting is the fact that beginning in 1945, the company became, in essence, a branch of the city's new All-American Football Conference (AAFC) team, the Cleveland Browns.

The owner of the cab company, Arthur "Mickey" McBride was also part owner of the Browns and one of the figures who helped establish the All American Conference as a rival to the National Football League. McBride had purportedly become interested in football in 1940 after watching a Notre Dame game. He was so keen about the sport that he tried to purchase the Cleveland Rams, the city's NFL franchise from 1937 to 1945. Unsuccessful, he secured the Cleveland franchise in the new AAFC. He also secured Paul Brown for head coach—a move that laid the foundation for a golden age of pro football in Cleveland.

Brown had an eye for the best talent and an ability to attract it to the Browns. Indeed, he was able to bring in more players than allowed—the roster then being limited to thirty-three players. Unwilling to part with the extras, he worked out a scheme with the team's co-owner. The extra players would become employees of the taxi company, but none would ever really drive a cab. Brown would funnel team funds to McBride. McBride would then cut paychecks for the players as company employees. When someone on the roster was injured, Brown simply needed to call a cab—that is to bring in one of McBride's so-called employees. It was a brilliant move and it led to terms that endure in pro football—Taxi Squad or Cab Squad—a concept born in Cleveland through the connivance of a brilliant football coach and an astute businessman who knew how to work the edges and whose love of football gave the city one of its most successful sports franchises.

Season tickets were not too expensive for Browns fans in 1948 and a winning team was a certainty.

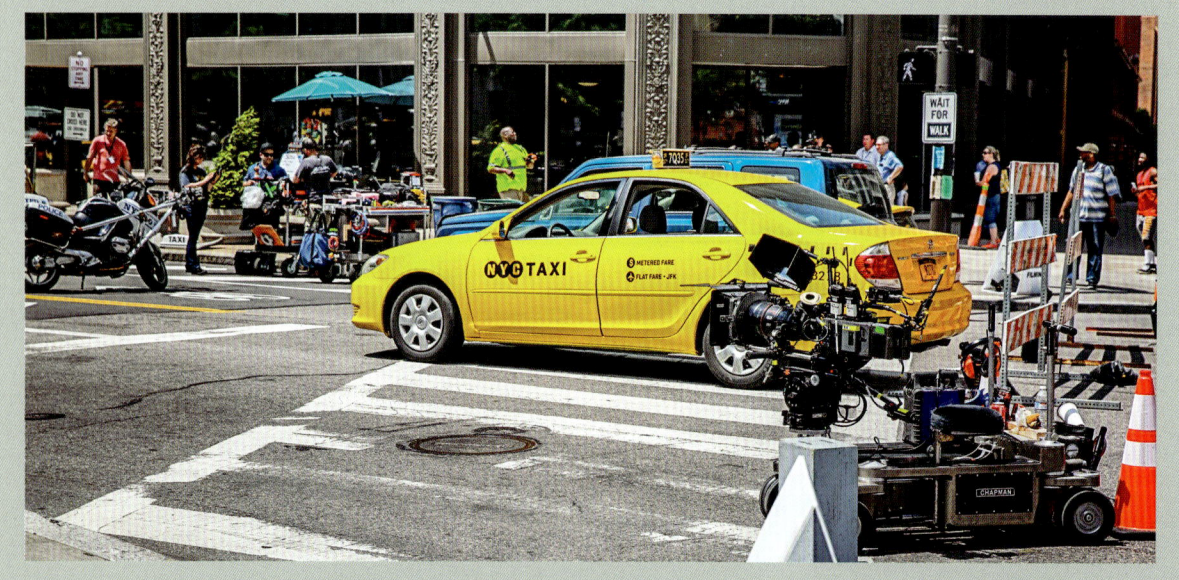

This NYC cab is poised for the shoot of a scene in *Fast 8*, **the latest in the** *Fast and Furious* **series, shot in Cleveland in May and June, 2016.**

70   CLEVELAND A to Z

CY YOUNG (1867–1955)

Scan to learn more

This image by noted Cleveland sports photographer, Louis Van Oeyen, shows the great Cy Young, then retired, at his home in Newcomerstown, Ohio.

Denton True "Cy" Young was not born in Cleveland, but he played baseball for Cleveland and that's all that counts! Young, the winningest pitcher in major league history, played for two Cleveland teams—the Spiders and the Naps. His story provides a good way to understand why baseball has been so important to the city.

Young first played professional ball for the Cleveland Spiders from 1890 to 1898, a former American Association team that had moved into the National League in 1889. The story of the Spiders has much to say about the ups and downs of professional baseball in Cleveland. They were an excellent team and won the National League's Temple Cup in 1895, which, in the years before the American League and the World Series, represented the pinnacle of baseball success. One of Young's teammates on the Spiders was Louis Sockalexis, a Native American from the Penobscot tribe who played for the team from 1897–1899. Some claim that the Cleveland Indians are named in honor of him, but that is disputable. What is not disputable is the sadness of Sockalexis's career in Cleveland. He started out phenomenally, but two years later his early promise was destroyed by alcohol and it was not helped by a management decision. In 1899 the Spiders' owner, Frank Robison, siphoned off its best players to the team he owned in St. Louis. Young was among those who left. Sockalexis was among those who remained, but he did not have to endure the season—he was cut after seven games. Perhaps it was a good thing as the team lost 134 games that season—still a record.

Despite this, baseball remained popular in Cleveland. Sandlot ball played by company, church, and fraternal teams was becoming a mainstay in the city and a training ground for many immigrant boys who wished to show their prowess in the sport. When the American League opened for business in 1901, the city secured a charter franchise. The team—first named the Blues, then the Broncos, and later in 1903, the Naps (after player-manager Napoleon LaJoie)—was popular. By the 1910s the city was baseball crazy. Over 100,000 people jammed into Brookside Park in 1915 to watch a championship game in which the local White Motors team was playing.

Young came "home" to Cleveland in 1909 when he joined the Naps. He stayed until 1911 when he moved to Boston where, the same year, he finished his professional career—his total wins were 511. Young lived long enough to see his former team win two World Series in 1920 and 1948. He was also alive in 1954 when the Indians secured the American League Pennant with a season record 111 wins. But the team then lost four straight games to the Giants in the Series. That, to many, in retrospect seemed the end of the team's great years, but the 1990s saw a burst of hope when several division titles were secured as well as a fourth, albeit unsuccessful, World Series appearance in 1997. In 2016 the team came close again, losing its World Series bid against the Chicago Cubs in the tenth inning of the seventh game.

Of course, everyone is still waiting and still hopeful despite the lack of a Series win over the past sixty-eight years. Despite the championship drought, there is some solace in knowing that four Cleveland pitchers have won the award named after one of the best players ever to wear a Cleveland uniform.

Standing just outside Progressive Field in 2016 are statues of pitching great Bob Feller, franchise home run leader Jim Thome, and American League color-barrier breaker Larry Doby.

THE ZOO

Scan to learn more

The Cleveland Zoo's first location in Wade Park was home to Miss Columbus when this postcard was issued in the early 1900s.

Arguably (if one considers taxidermy), the first zoo in Cleveland was within a small building on Rockwell Avenue (near Public Square), where Leonard Case Jr., his brother William, and a group of friends met in the 1840s to discuss a variety of topics ranging from geology to history and natural history. It was dubbed the "Ark," given the number of stuffed birds and other specimens within the rooms. It would serve as the progenitor of several current Cleveland cultural organizations.

Clevelanders would have to wait four decades for a living zoo—and when they received it, in 1882, it was stocked with deer. Located in Wade Park, it slowly acquired other attractions. By the early 1900s, it housed wildcats, a variety of birds, an alligator (which had previously resided in a pond on Public Square), polar bears, lions, and sea lions. It was quite a menagerie for a small park and a noisy neighbor for the upscale Wade Allotment residences, then being envisioned just across East Boulevard from the cages and ponds. In 1907 it began a gradual move to Brookside Reservation on the city's West Side to a site along Big Creek, which it occupies today. It completed the move in 1916, just as the new Cleveland Museum of Art opened in Wade Park. One could make much of this transition: high culture and high society replacing a popular attraction that goes west of the river in order to thrive.

That, however, would be a mistake because part of the zoo site eventually became the home of the Cleveland Museum of Natural History, which moved to Wade Park in 1958. It is one of the institutions that can claim the Ark as its origin. The Western Reserve Historical Society, another "child of the ark," is just across the street and it, ironically, has part of its operations in two of the grand homes that would have been within earshot of the grunts, growls, and squeals of the Wade Park Zoo. Visit either today and you will find them crowded with children and families, just as the first zoo had been.

It's a connection that becomes even more palpable at the outdoor areas of the Natural History Museum where visitors can see living animals in the newly (2016) reconfigured and expanded Perkins Wildlife Center, which serves as a reminder of the previous "residents" who went west to Brookside a century ago.

The 1956 Viktor Schreckengost mastodon and mammoth sculptures that once adorned the pachyderm building at the Cleveland Metroparks Zoo now are part of the Cleveland Museum of Natural History at the East Boulevard entrance to University Circle

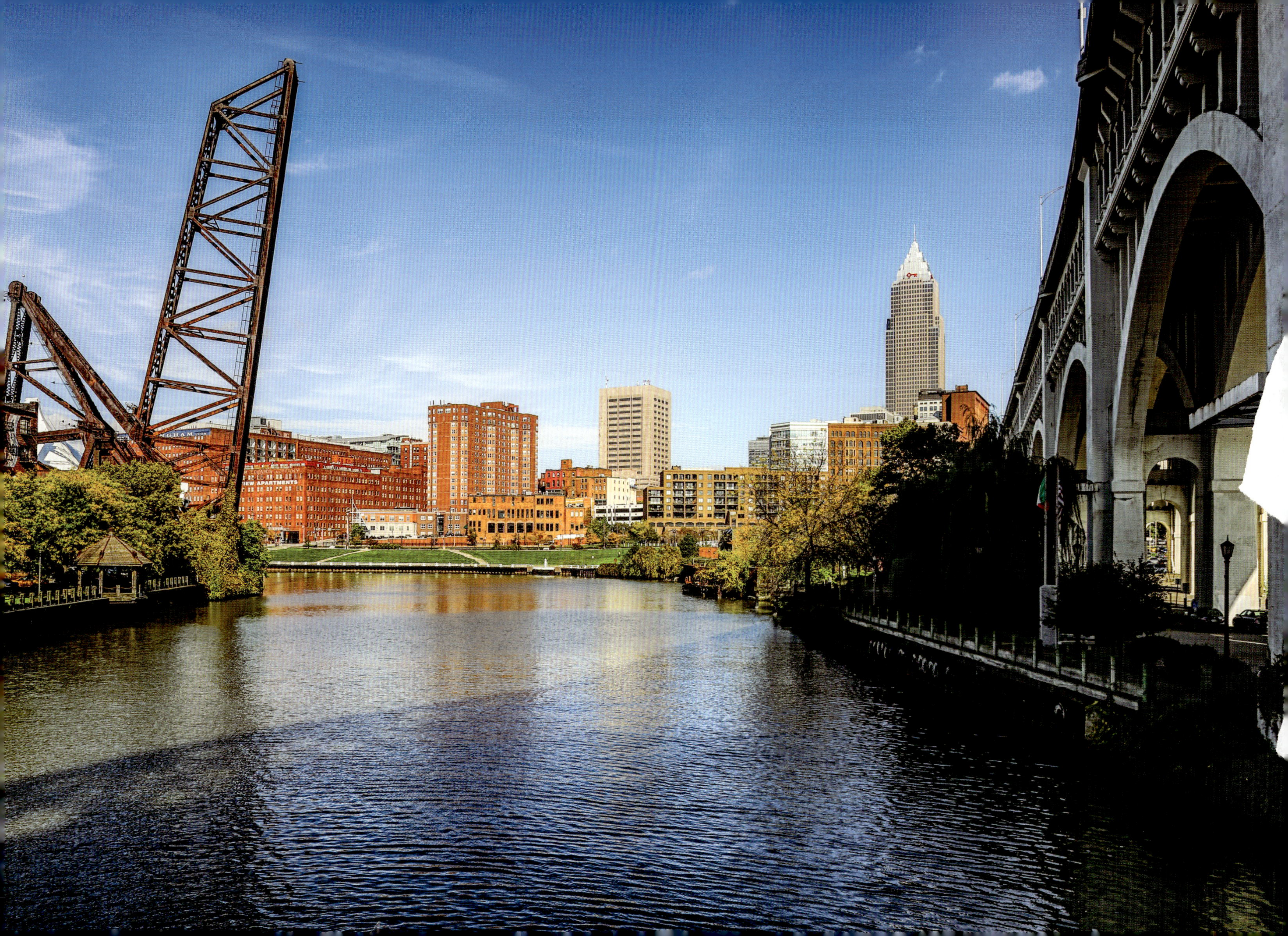

INDEX

A Christmas Story, 9
Adams, Almeda, 12
African American Cultural Garden, 11
African Americans, 8, 24, 40, 43, 44, 55, 61
Agora, 1, 47
Air Force One, 47
All American Football Conference, 50
Allen, Florence Ellinwood, 56
Alsbacher, Moses, 2
Alta Social Settlement, 54
American Cultural Garden, 11
American Indians (see Native Americans)
American Red Cross, 39
American Shipbuilding, 51
Anderson, Ernie, 45
Andrews, Samuel, 3
Antioch Baptist Church, 8
Ark ("the Ark"), 72
ART AND MUSIC, 1, 12, 32, 34, 39, 51, 66, 69
Art's Seafood, 8
Azeri Cultural Garden, 11
Baseball, 71
Baseball, Sandlot, 71
Basketball, 39
Battle of Fallen Timbers, 43
Beach Boys, 19
Bedford Historical Society, 22

Bedford, Ohio, 22
Beechbrook, 12
Berlin Heights, Ohio, 48, 55
Bertman's Original Ballpark Mustard, 41
Big Creek, 72
Big Italy, 5
Bildungsverein Eintract, 21
Birdtown, 4
Birns, Shondor, 26
Black Hawk, 30
Black Nativity, 32
Bleecker, Katherine, 46
Bohannon, James, 46
Bohn, Ernest J., 35
Boiardi, Hector (Ettore), 5
Bolton, Frances Payne, 12
Bomber Plant, 29
Bourke-White, Margaret, 62
Boyd Funeral Home, 8
Bratenahl, 47
Bratenahl Place, 35
Bridge War, 6
Bridges, 6
British Cultural Garden, 11
Brooklyn Township, 43
Brooklyn, 24
Brookside Park, 71

Brookside Reservation, 72
Brown, Paul, 70
Brunner, Arnold, 38
Brush, Charles F., 39
Buffalo Road, 18
Burke Brook, 23, 33
Burning River Ale, 7
Burning River Fest, 68
Burton, Harold H., 42
Cab Squad, 70
Canterbury, Connecticut, 10
Capone, Al, 42
Captain America: The Winter Soldier, 47
Carabelli, Joseph, 37
Carling Brewing Company of Canada, 46
Carrere, John, 38
Carter, Lorenzo, 68
Case School of Applied Sciences, 63
Case Western Reserve University, 1, 12, 36, 37, 63
Case, Leonard, Jr., 72
"Cat Nation," 17
Cedar Avenue, 8
Cedar Gardens, 8
Cedar Hill, 27
Cedar Point, 19
Central Avenue, 8

Central High School, 25, 54
Chagrin River Valley, 16, 47
Charles II, King of England, Scotland, and Ireland, 67
Cholera Epidemic (1832), 68
Cigliano, Jan, 3
Civil Rights Movement, 61
Civil War (American), 54
Clay, Henry, 22
Cleaveland, Moses, 10, 18, 30
Cleveland Academy of Natural Sciences, 22
Cleveland Advertiser, 10
Cleveland American Indian Center, 30
Cleveland Arena, 39
Cleveland Auto Show, 29
Cleveland Board of Education Building, 38
Cleveland Botanical Garden, 66
Cleveland Browns, 36, 47, 50, 61, 70
Cleveland Buckeyes, 36
Cleveland Call and Post, 69
Cleveland Cinematheque, 47
Cleveland City Hall, 38
Cleveland Cultural Gardens, 11, 12
Cleveland Food Co Op., 28
Cleveland Gazette and Commercial Register, 17
Cleveland Heights, 24, 27, 54
Cleveland Hopkins Airport, 29
Cleveland Indians, 30, 36, 47 61, 71

Cleveland Institute of Art, 47
Cleveland International Film Festival, 47
Cleveland League of Women Voters, 56
Cleveland Metroparks, 20
Cleveland Metroparks Zoo, 72
Cleveland Museum of Art, 34, 66, 72
Cleveland Museum of Natural History, 66, 72
Cleveland Naps, 71
Cleveland Orchestra, 12
Cleveland Press, 48
Cleveland Protestant Orphan Asylum, 12
Cleveland Public Library, 61
Cleveland Rams, 70
Cleveland Recording Company, 69
Cleveland Spiders, 71
Cleveland State University, 1
Cleveland Style Polka Hall of Fame, 51
Cleveland Union Stockyards, 65
Cleveland Union Terminal, 33, 64
Club Isabella, 1
Cole, Allen, 8
College Equal Suffrage League, 56
Collinwood, 24, 51
Columbian Exposition (1893), 38
Columbus Street Bridge, 6
Consumers League, 56
Corlett, 24
Crawford Auto Museum, 46

Croatian Cultural Garden, 12, 12
Cuyahoga County Courthouse, 38
Cuyahoga Falls, Ohio, 13
Cuyahoga River Fire, 7, 13
Cuyahoga River, 6, 7, 13, 20, 27, 33, 40, 68
Czechs, 59
Darling, Charles, 47
Das Echo, 21
Democratic Party Steer Roast, 19
Ditka, Mike, 50
DIVERSITY, 2, 4, 5, 8, 11, 21, 30, 32, 34, 37, 40, 44, 45, 49, 51, 59, 61, 68, 69
Doan Brook, 14, 23, 63, 66
Doan, Nathanial, 14
Doby, Larry, 61
Downtown, 15
East Bank Project, 20
East Cleveland, 24, 54, 61
East Side vs. West Side, 6
East Technical High School, 44
Edgehill Road, 27
Edgewater Park, 16, 57
Emerald Necklace, 16
ENVIRONMENT AND LANDSCAPE, 7, 11, 13, 14, 16, 17, 20, 23, 27, 33, 35, 38, 40, 52, 57, 63, 65, 66, 68
Environmental Protection Agency, 7
Erie Street Cemetery, 17

Erie Street, 17
Euclid Avenue Baptist Church, 54
Euclid Avenue, 18, 66
Euclid Beach Park, 19
Euclid Beach Riot, 19
Euclid Tavern, 18
Euclid Township, 18
Fairfax Planning District, 8
Fairmount Junior High School, 44
Feast of the Assumption, 37
Feller, Bob, 36
"Fence War," 52
First Baptist Church, 12
First Energy Stadium, 41,
Flats, 20, 54
Fleet Avenue, 59
Flora Stone Mather College, 12
FOOD AND DRINK, 5, 7, 41, 49, 46
Football, 50
Forest Hill, 54
Fort Huntington Park, 44
Fortune (magazine), 62
Fortune Cookie (film), 47
Franklin Avenue, 43
Franklin Castle, 21
Franklin Circle, 16
Franklin Club, 48
Franklin, Benjamin, 13

Freed, Alan, 39
Gambling, 26
Garfield Monument, 35
Garfield, James A., 35
Garlick, Theodatus, 22
Geauga County, 13
George, Henry, 25, 31
Germania (German newspaper), 69
Germans, 9, 21
GI Bill, 45
Giardino d'Italia, 5
Giddings Avenue, 23
Giddings Brook, 23
Giddings Elementary School, 23
Giddings, Charles M., 23
Glenville Shootout, 24
Glenville, 24
Global Center for Health Innovation, 38
Goethe, Johann, 34
Gordon, William J., 14, 16
Great Depression, 16, 29, 35, 42, 64
Great Lakes Brewing Company, 42, 68
Great Lakes Exposition, 42
Great Lakes Science Center, 51
Great Lakes Towing Company, 7
Great Migration, 44, 61
Green Springs, Ohio, 48
Group Plan, 38

Gwinn estate, 47
Haddon, Britton, 62
Halles Department Store, 15
Hanna (Leonard) Mansion, 57
Hanna, Leonard Jr., 32
Hanna, Marcus Alonzo, 25
Harvard Avenue, 26
Harvard Club, 26
Harvard Denison Bridge, 65
Hauser, Elizabeth, 56
Haywood, "Big Bill," 21
Heights (the), 27
Hessler Court, 28
Hessler Road, 28
Higbee's Department Store, 5, 15
Hispanic Immigrants, 69
Hockey (Ice), 17, 39
Hough, 36
Hughes, Adella Prentiss, 12
Hughes, Langston, 32
Hulett Ore Unloades, 68
Humphrey Family, 19
Hungarians, 34
I-X Center, 29
Indian Cultural Garden, 11
INDUSTRY/BUSINESS, 1, 3, 4, 6, 8, 15, 20, 26, 29, 40, 49, 50, 51, 54, 58, 62, 64, 66, 69, 70

Irish, 68
Irishtown Bend, 20
Isle of Man, 51
JACK Casino, 9, 15, 26
Jackowa (neighborhood), 59
Jackson, Andrew, 22
Jean's Fun House, 58
Jelliffe, Rowena, 32
Jelliffe, Russell, 32
Jethro, Sam "The Jet," 36
Jewish Community, 2, 24, 43
Joc-O-Sot, 30
Johnson, Hiram, 31
Johnson, Tom L., 25, 31, 34
Karamu House, 32
Karlin (neighborhood), 59
Kennedy, John F., 19
Kid from Cleveland (film), 47
King, Don, 26
Kingsbury Run, 20, 33
Kingsbury, James, 33
Kirtland, Ohio, 55
Kiss, 1
Kluber, Cory, 71
Korean War, 29
Kosciuszko, Tadeusz, 34
Kossuth Statue, 34

Kossuth, Louis, 34
Krakowa (neighborhood), 59
Kremlin, 21
LaJoie, Napoleon, 71
Lake Erie Monsters, 17
Lake Erie, 17
Lake View Cemetery, 35, 37, 42, 54, 64, 66
Lakeview Terrace, 35
Lakewood Gold Coast, 35
Lakewood, 4, 24, 64
Las Vegas, Nevada, 58
"Laughing Sal," 19
League Park, 36, 47
Lee, Cliff, 71
Life (magazine), 62
Little Italy, 28, 35, 37, 54
LoConti, Henry J., 1
Lomond Association, 55
Luce, Henry, 62
Ludlow Association, 55
M. A. Hanna Company, 25
Mall, 38
Manx, 51
Marconi Medical Systems, 69
Martin Luther King Jr. Boulevard, 11, 12
Mather (Samuel) Mansion, 57
May Company, 9, 15

Mayfield Road, 27
Mayfield Village, 60
McBride, Arthur "Mickey," 70
McKinley, William, 25
Means, Russell, 30
Merwin's Wharf, 20
Metropolitan Theater, 47
Michael Stanley Band, 1
Miles Park, 16
Miller, William, 55
Millerites, 55
Millionaires' Row, 3, 18, 23, 31, 43
Mintz, Leo, 39
Mob Museum (Las Vegas), 58
Mobbed Up, 58
Moondog Coronation Ball, 39
Morgan Run 23, 33, 59
Morgan, Garrett, 40
Mormons, 55
Motley, Marion, 61
Mound Street, 59
Mounds Club, 26
Municipal Stadium, 36, 41
Music Settlement, 12
Musical Arts Association, 12
Mustard, 41
National Carbon Company, 4

National League of Women Voters, 56
National Museum of the Great Lakes (Toledo), 51
Nationalities Broadcasting Association, 69
Native Americans, 17, 30, 43, 59, 67, 71
NEIGHBORHOODS AND SUBURBS, 4, 8, 15, 18, 20, 24, 27, 28, 37, 43, 45, 55, 58, 59, 63, 65, 68
Ness, Eliot, 26, 33, 42
New Connecticut, 67
Newburgh Heights, 26
Newburgh Township, 33
Newspaper Annie, 48
Niagara, Oghema (Chief Thunderwater), 30
North, Colonel Oliver, 61
Northwest Ordinance of 1787, 67
Northwest Territory, 67
Nottingham, 24
Ohio and Erie Canal, 13, 20, 43, 68
Ohio City, 24, 43
Old Stone (First Presbyterian) Church, 26
One University Circle, 63
Orange Village, 60
Out and About with Winsor French, 58
Outhwaite Homes, 61
Owens, Jesse, 8, 44
Parma Heights, 27
Parma, 27, 45, 49
"Parma Place," 45

Peake, George, 43
Peerless Motor Car Company, 46
Penton Publishing, 62
Perkins, Anna, 48
Perkins, Joseph, 16
Perils of Society, 47
Perry, Gaylord, 71
Pettibone Club, 26
Picker X Ray Corp., 69
Pierogies, 49
Pittsburgh Road, 50
Pittsburgh, 50
Platt, Lew, 39
Play House Settlement, 32
Poles, 4, 45, 59
POLITICS 19, 24, 25, 31, 34, 61
Polka, 49, 51
PolyOne Corporation, 25
POPULAR CULTURE 1, 8, 9, 19, 26, 28, 39, 51, 58, 72
Praha (neighborhood), 59
Prentiss, Alta Rockefeller, 54
Preservation Movement, 43
Progressive Era, 16, 31
Progressive Field, 41
Public Auditorium, 38
Public Housing, 35, 61

Public Square, 9, 10, 16, 26, 31, 34, 38, 48, 52, 72
Quayle and Sons, 51
Quayle, Thomas, 51
Ralph Perkins II Wildlife Center & Woods Garden, 72
Ray, James Earl, 61
Record Rendezvous, 39
Reed, John, 21
Regionalism, 24
Republic Steel Company, 65
Republican National Convention 1936, 42
Riley, Charles, 44
Robison, Frank, 71
Rock and roll, 39, 51
Rockefeller Building, 54
Rockefeller Park, 11, 14, 16
Rockefeller Park, 54
Rockefeller Physics Building (CWRU), 54
Rockefeller, John D., 3, 16, 25, 33, 35, 37, 54
Rockefeller, Laura Celestia (Cettie), 54
Rocky River Valley, 16
Roosevelt, Theodore, 31
Rouse, Rebecca, 12
Rove, Karl, 25
Roxy Burlesque Theater, 58
Russo, Anthony, 47
Russo, Joe, 47
Ruth, Babe, 36

Ruthenberg, Charles, 21
Sabathia, CC, 71
Sauk Tribe, 30
Schiller, Friedrich, 34
Schuster, Joe, 24
Schwan, Rev. Heinrich, 9
Severance, Elisabeth, 12
Severance, John Long, 12
Severance Hall, 12, 47
"Sex radicals," 55
Shaker Heights, 24, 27, 33, 55, 64
Shaker Square, 15
Shakespeare Garden, 11
Sherwin Williams, 56
Sherwin, Belle, 56
"Shock Theater," 45
Shoreway, 57
Short Vincent Street, 58
Siegel, Jerry, 24
Slavic Village, 23, 45, 59
Slovaks, 4, 34
Slovenian Cultural Garden, 11
Slovenians, 51
Socialists, 21
Sockalexis, Louis, 71
Sokoloff, Nikolai, 12
Soldiers Aid Society, 12

Solon, Ohio, 60
SOM Center Road, 60
Sorosis, 48
Southgate, 15
Southside Johnny, 1
Spafford, Amos, 52
SPORTS, 24, 30, 36, 41, 44, 50, 70, 71
Springsteen, Bruce, 1
St. Alexis Hospital, 48
St. Cyril and Methodius Church, 4
St. Gaudens, August, 25
St. James AME Church, 8
Stadium Mustard, 41
Standard Oil, 3, 33, 54
Steffans, Lincoln, 31
Sterling Lindner, 15
Sterling School, 23
Stinchcomb, William, 16
Stokes Boulevard, 14, 63
Stokes, Carl, 44, 61
Stokes, Charles, 61
Stokes, Louis, 61
Stokes, Louise, 61
Stone, Amasa, 63
Strongsville, 54
Suburbs, 24, 45, 55
Superior Viaduct, 20
Superman, 24

Tank Plant, 29
Taxi Squad, 70
Taylors Department Store, 15
The Age of Freedom, 55
The Good Time Coming, 55
The Ohio State University, 44
The Untouchables, 42
Thorman, Simson, 2
Tiedemann, Hannes, 21
Time (magazine), 61, 62
Torso Murders, 33, 42
Torso Murders, 42
Treaty of Fort Industry, 43
Treaty of Greenville, 10, 43
Tremont, 43, 45
Trotting (races), 24
Tubbs Jones, Stephanie, 12
"Turnpike War," 50
Ukrainians, 4, 45
Underground Railroad, 32
Union Club, 47
United Society of Believers in Christ's Second Appearance, 55
University Circle, 14, 25, 61, 63, 66
Val's in the Alley, 8
Van Sweringen Brothers, 55
Van Sweringen, Mantis James, 33, 64
Van Sweringen, Oris Paxton, 33, 64

Vincent Street, 58
Vinegar Hill, 65
Visiting Nurse Association 56
Wade Allotment, 66, 72
Wade Oval, 66
Wade Park, 72
Wade, Jeptha Homer, 14, 16, 66
Wade, Jeptha Homer II ("Homer"), 66
Walworth Run, 33
War Memorial Fountain, 38
Warren, Moses, 18
Warszawa (neighborhood), 59
Washington, Booker T., 11
Washington, George, 13
Water, 40
WELW, 69
Wendy Park, 68
West Shoreway, 40
West Side Market, 43
Western Reserve (Connecticut Western Reserve), 10, 13, 60, 67
Western Reserve College, 63
Western Reserve Historical Society, 1, 8, 19, 31, 34, 40, 42, 47, 48, 66
Western Union, 66
Whiskey Island, 68
White Motors Baseball Team, 71
White, Stanford, 57

WHWN, 69
William G. Mather (ore carrier), 51
Willis, Bill, 61
Windham, Connecticut, 10
Winton Hotel, 5
WJW, 39
WMMS, 1
WNZN (Lorain, Ohio), 69
Wolf, Frederick, 69
Women Suffrage Party of Greater Cleveland, 56
Works Progress Administration, 16, 57
World War I, 56
Wright, Alonzo, 8
WXEN, 69
WZAK, 69
Yale University, 10
Yankovic, Frankie, 51
Yellow Cab Company, 70
Young, Denton True "Cy," 71
Yugoslav Cultural Garden, 12
Zapis, Xenophon, 69
Zion Evangelical Lutheran Church, 9

The Grand Opening Ceremony of the transformed Public Square took place in time for the Republican National Convention.

TABLE OF PLATES

Plate 1 – Foreword Making traditional cabbage rolls at R&K Sausage, a fourth-generation family-owned company founded by Joseph Radecki in 1917. Located in the heart of Slavic Village, R&K specializes in ethnic Polish cuisine.

Plate 2 – Agora The entrance to the 1,800-seat Agora Theatre, with its storied history, is across the lobby from the Agora Ballroom with a standing-room-only capacity of 500.

Plate 3 – Moses Alsbacher The Maltz Museum of Jewish Heritage—founded in collaboration with the Maltz Family Foundation, the Jewish Federation of Cleveland, the Temple-Tifereth Israel, and the Western Reserve Historical Society—is designed to introduce visitors to Jewish heritage in America. A number of Alsbacher artifacts are on display in the museum's galleries, including the Alsbacher document, written Lazarus Kohn to Moses and Yetta Alsbacher in 1839, instructing the Alsbacher party always to remember their heritage.

Plate 4 – Andrews's Folly Looking east on Chester Avenue across what was once the estate of Samuel Andrews, when Euclid Avenue properties extended north to Perkins Avenue. In the left foreground is the former Towell Cadillac dealership, and subsequently the Cleveland branch of the Cadillac Motor Car Company, where Frederick C. Crawford opened the Thompson Products Auto Album in August 1943. The museum of antique automobiles remained at this location until the Frederick C. Crawford Auto-Aviation Museum opened in University Circle as part of the Western Reserve Historical Society.

Plate 5 – Birdtown Churches representing the ethnicities of the immigrants who moved to the Lakewood neighborhood to work at nearby National Carbon Company.

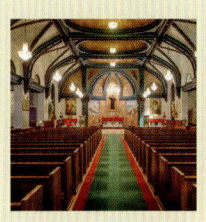

Plate 6 – Hector (Ettore) Boiardi On Carnegie Avenue, just east of the former Hotel Winton, stands Saint Maron's, a Maronite church serving Syrian and Lebanese worshipers since 1939, formerly the home of the congregation of Saint Anthony's, which built the red-brick Romanesque church in 1904 to serve the Italian immigrants of Big Italy in Cleveland's Haymarket area. By 1938 the members of the congregation had largely moved out of Big Italy, and the remaining congregants merged with Saint Bridget's, an Irish congregation. Today the Haymarket area is home to the Gateway Sports and Entertainment Complex.

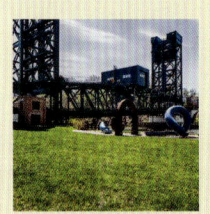

Plate 7 – The Bridge War The fifth span of the Columbus Street Bridge, originally constructed in 1836, was installed in 2014 and serves as a beautiful backdrop to the Metroparks' Rivergate Park, which features Merwin's Wharf, a full-service restaurant. Named for Nobel Merwin, one of the flat's earliest tavern owners, Merwin's Wharf offers a spectacular view of the Cuyahoga River and Irishtown Bend from its patio.

Plate 8 – Burning River Lit during the 2013 National Senior Games, the flaming cauldron stands as a symbol of Cleveland's industrial past and technological future. Designed by Ron Payto, crafted by Mark Benton and Stephen Manka, and intended for installation along the Cuyahoga River to celebrate the river's rebirth following the fire of July 1969, the piece has found a home on Cleveland's Mall as a part of the city's public art collection.

Plate 9 – Cedar Avenue One of the iconic structures is Antioch Baptist Church, the former home of the Bolton Avenue Presbyterian Church, which merged with Calvary Presbyterian Church in 1923. The African American Baptist congregation, the second oldest such church in Cleveland, was formed in 1893 and moved to its present location in 1924. Through its nonprofit agency, the Antioch Development Corporation, the church is actively addressing the social, economic, and spiritual needs of the community.

Plate 10 – Christmas Stories Built in 1895, the "Christmas Story House," located on Cleveland's near West Side, was used only for the exterior scenes of the classic movie. The interior, however, now matches that of the house in the film. Ralphie's Red Ryder BB gun is leaning against the fireplace, and the toys around the Christmas tree were among those in Higbee's Department Store window on Public Square.

Plate 11 – Moses Cleaveland The towering statue of Gen. Moses Cleaveland was given to the city by the Early Settlers Association in 1888. Previously standing on the southwest quadrant of Cleveland's Public Square in front of what is now the Renaissance Hotel, the statue was restored during the transformation of Public Square. It now faces north on the south side of the square, opposite the statue of Tom L. Johnson (see Plate 32).

Plate 12 – Cleveland Cultural Gardens The American Legion Peace Garden was dedicated on September 20, 1936. One section, the Garden of Nations, contains a vault with the inscription, "Here in soil from historic shrines of the Nations of the World, are planted trees to create the American Legion Peace Gardens. May the intermingled soil of the nations symbolize the united effort of their peoples as they advance to a better understanding." Similarly, the Garden of States contains soil from each of the fifty states.

Plate 13 – The Cleveland Orchestra In contrast to the Neoclassical exterior, Severance Hall's Grand Foyer is in the Egyptian Revival style. Fourteen murals by Else Vick Shaw, a member of the Cleveland School of artists, depict the origins of music. As you enjoy the murals, do not forget to look for the brass screw embedded among the marble chips of the terrazzo floor. Legend has it that this is the only imperfection in the Grand Foyer.

Plate 14 – Cuyahoga River The freighter *Manistee* snakes its way through the tight turns of the crooked river as it heads upriver to the steel mills to unload its cargo of coal, limestone, or iron ore from the Superior Range. Before the days of bow thrusters, the cargo was unloaded by massive Hulett Unloaders on Whiskey Island, near the mouth of the river, to be delivered to the mills in rail cars. Self-unloading freighters spelled the end for the Hulett Unloaders (see Plate 69).

Plate 15 – Doan Brook The brook that cuts through public parklands on its way to Lake Erie originates on a private country club, five miles to the southeast. After flowing through the man-made Shaker Lakes, the brook cuts through the gorge where sandstone was once quarried. As the brook became a focal point for the parks, it was confined in channels. Today the process has begun to return the brook to its natural, pre-channelized look.

Plate 16 – Downtown From the roof of the former Breuer Tower, now The 9 on East 9th Street, this photo shows Euclid Avenue, including, left to right, the Carl B. Stokes U.S. District Court House (2002), the Terminal Tower (1930), 200 Public Square (formerly BP Building, 1987), and Key Tower (1992). In the background are Lake Erie and the Lakewood Gold Coast.

Plate 17 – Emerald Necklace Established as a golf club in 1921, Acacia Country Club occupied as many as 300 acres at the northeast corner of Cedar and Richmond Roads in Lyndhurst. Aggressively sought by developers, the property, then consisting of 176 acres, was purchased by the Conservation Fund in December 2012 and transferred to the Cleveland Metroparks. The long, slow process of natural restoration is under way.

Plate 18 – Erie Gamaliel Fenton, a veteran of the Revolutionary War and the War of 1812, was buried in the Erie Street Cemetery after his death during the cholera epidemic of 1849. The cemetery, which bears the original name of East 9th Street, replaced an informal community burial ground south of Public Square in 1826. The Erie Street Cemetery is the resting place of Lorenzo Carter, Cleveland's first permanent settler (see Plate 68), and Chief Joc-O-Sot, chief of the Mesquakie tribe (see Plate 31). Of the 168 veterans who are buried in the Erie Street Cemetery, 98 fought in the Civil War.

Plate 19 – Euclid The oldest building still standing on its original site in the city of Cleveland is the Dunham Tavern Museum on Euclid Avenue. Built in 1824, its owners, Rufus and Jane Pratt Dunham, operated a tavern and stagecoach stop for travelers on the Buffalo-Cleveland Road. Heavy car and bus traffic now traverse the road that once was known as Millionaires' Row, and the Tavern has been a museum since 1941.

Plate 20 – Euclid Beach Many who visited the Euclid Beach amusement park did so by riding one of several streetcars. Trolley Car #1218, built by the G. C. Kuhlman Car Co. in 1914, was first operated by the Cleveland Railway Co., and took many fun-seekers to and from Euclid Beach. The trolley car was later leased to the Van Sweringen brothers' Cleveland Interurban Railroad, where it provided transportation between Shaker Heights and Terminal Tower. Car #1218 was retired in 1960, and Euclid Beach "closed for the season" in 1969. The trolley car can be seen at the Illinois Railway Museum.

Plate 21 – The Flats The key to the current renaissance of the Flats may be seen in the cross section of purposes depicted in this image, ranging from offices, hotels, condominiums, apartments, restaurants, bars, entertainment, and recreation. The Nautica Entertainment Complex and Greater Cleveland Aquarium anchor the west bank, while the Flats East Bank, a mixed-use neighborhood, anchors the east side of the river. Downriver, the Cleveland Rowing Foundation is developing Rivergate Park.

Plate 22– Franklin Castle After years of failed starts, fires, and narrowly escaping demolition, Franklin Castle is being beautifully restored to its stature as a showplace on Franklin Avenue. Architectural details, beautiful in their simplicity, are being faithfully reproduced. Missing marble is being carefully matched and replaced.

Plate 23 – Theodatus Garlick A short walk from Garlick's home is Bedford's Public Square, with memorials to American war veterans and Baseball Hall of Famer, Elmer Flick. In 1837, Hezekiah Dunham and his wife Clarissa donated three acres of land to the Village of Bedford with the stipulation that it be "used as a public square forever." Facing the square from the south are the 1892 Baptist church, now used as a community hall, and the 1874 town hall, now home to the Bedford Historical Society.

Plate 24 – Giddings Avenue A short stretch of East 71st Street, between Wade Park and Superior Avenue, still bears the Giddings name. The intersection of Giddings and Wade Park is the microcosm of a neighborhood in transition; among recently constructed townhouse developments are a vacant, vandalized building on one corner, a renovated store on another, and a repurposed gas station on a third.

Plate 25 – Glenville The birthplace of Superman, the boyhood home of Jerry Siegel, where he and Joe Shuster spent hours creating the Man of Steel, the world's first superhero. Today, Jefferson and Hattie May Gray have transformed their home into a shrine honoring Glenville's three hometown heroes, Jerry Siegel, Joe Shuster, and Clark Kent.

Plate 26 – Marcus Alonzo Hanna Three years after the death of Marcus A. Hanna, a monument was erected just south of the Wade Lagoon, stating, "By Friends and Fellow Citizens Commemorating His Efforts for Peace Between Capital and labor, His Useful Citizenship and Distinguished Public Service."

Plate 27 – The Harvard Club There is no sign of the Harvard Club, either at the first location at 3111 Harvard or the second, at 4209 Harvard. Older residents have memories of the illicit activity of the past, especially when the shifts changed at the factories that lined the south side of Harvard Avenue.

Plate 28 – The Heights The children's playhouse is one of three buildings and beautiful stone walls and iron gates remaining on the former Briggs Estate that occupied a 5.5-acre city block in Cleveland Heights from 1909 to 1965. When the thirty-room, Tudor-style mansion was demolished, it was replaced by four, four-unit Frank Lloyd Wright–esque condominiums. The Mornington Lane Condominiums are consistent with the move from sprawling mansions that continues throughout the Heights.

Plate 29 – Hessler The residence of Emory M. Hessler and the intersection of Hessler Road and Hessler Court, designed by Cleveland Architect George Kauffman, was built in 1900. It is said that the house originally stood at the intersection of Ford Drive and Hessler Road before being moved east to its present location. Each May, more than 10,000 people flock to the Hessler Street Fair for crafts, poetry, face painting, and balloon animals.

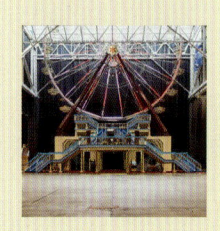

Plate 30 – I-X Center The Ferris wheel, the most recognizable feature of the I-X Center, debuted in 1992. The Ferris wheel stands 125 feet tall and is the centerpiece of the building. The top of the wheel, enclosed in a glass atrium, rises approximately 35 feet above the main roof and can be seen for miles. It operates during most shows and at one time was the tallest indoor Ferris wheel.

Plate 31 – Joc-O-Sot Before his death in August 1844, the member of the Sauk tribe made known his wish to be buried near his Central Plains home in Minnesota or Wisconsin. When he died in Cleveland, he was buried in the Erie Street Cemetery. His tombstone is said to have been broken by his rage at being buried so far from his ancestral land.

Plate 32 – Tom L. Johnson During the transformation of Public Square, the statues of Moses Cleaveland and Tom Johnson were restored to their original beauty. With the closing of Ontario Street, Moses Cleaveland was relocated to the south side of the Square, facing north, up Ontario to the County Courthouse. Tom Johnson sits on the north side of the Square with his back to the Courthouse, looking past Moses Cleaveland.

Plate 33 – Karamu House One of the homes in which the black poet, playwright, novelist, and lecturer Langston Hughes grew up. Like Ernest Hemingway, whose start was in his third-floor bedroom in Oak Park, Illinois, Hughes got his in his third-floor bedroom of this house, where he wrote his first play, *The Golden Piece,* in 1921.

Plate 34 – Kingsbury Run Cleveland's only suspension bridge was designed by Case Western Reserve professor of engineering Fred L. Plummer and built by the Van Sweringen brothers in 1931. It is a 680-foot-long pedestrian footbridge spanning Kingsbury Run, above the former Shaker Rapid Transit car barns, and connecting two ends of Sidaway Avenue—one in the Polish American neighborhood of Slavic Village, and the other in Garden Valley, an African American neighborhood. The bridge has been unused since it was vandalized during civil unrest in 1966.

Plate 35 – Kossuth Statue On the south side of Euclid Avenue, between Stearns Road and Martin Luther King Jr. Drive and looking across Euclid to the site of the M. A. Hanna Statue (see Plate 26).

Plate 36 – Lake Views The view from one of the highest points at Lake View Cemetery, looking across the graves of some of the city's citizens and across the treetops to Lake Erie.

Plate 37 – League Park Beautifully restored after years of neglect, League Park looks small. But stand behind home plate and it is a long, long way to the center field fence—420 feet, to be exact. Stand at home plate and imagine being The Babe, waiting for the pitch that would be his 500th home run, or "Rapid Robert" Feller, standing on the mound, staring down the opposing batter. The restored League Field has brought a sense of pride to the neighborhood— and a fresh coat of paint to the fronts of some of the adjacent homes.

Plate 38 – Little Italy Looking east on Mayfield Road into the heart of Little Italy, with the iconic Holy Rosary Church and the flags of the United States and Italy.

Plate 39 – The Mall A view of the south end of the Mall, with the Fountain of Eternal Life, also known as *Peace Arising from the Flames of War,* which was dedicated on May 30, 1964, to the memory of those from Greater Cleveland who died serving their country in World War II and in the Korean War. In the background is 200 Public Square. Completed in 1985, the forty-five-story office tower was home to Standard Oil of Ohio and was renamed BP America Tower in 1987. Today it is known as the Huntington Bank Building.

Plate 40 – Moondog Coronation Ball The original "Moondog" died in Palm Springs, California, in 1965 and was buried in Hartsdale, New York. In 2002, Alan Freed's remains were put on display at the Rock and Roll Hall of Fame, where they remained until 2014. Today his resting place is in Lake View Cemetery, appropriately enough, beneath a jukebox.

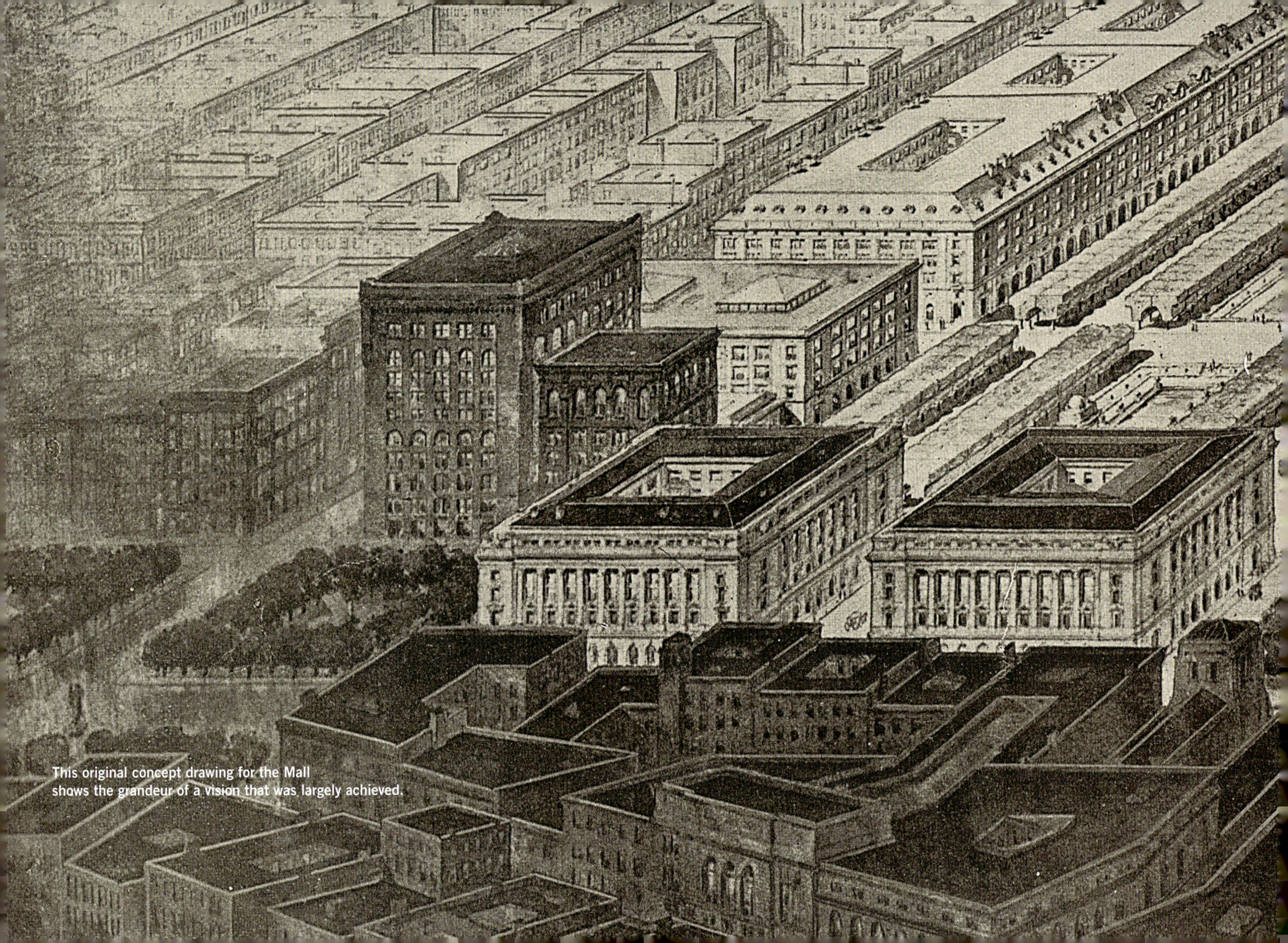

This original concept drawing for the Mall
shows the grandeur of a vision that was largely achieved.

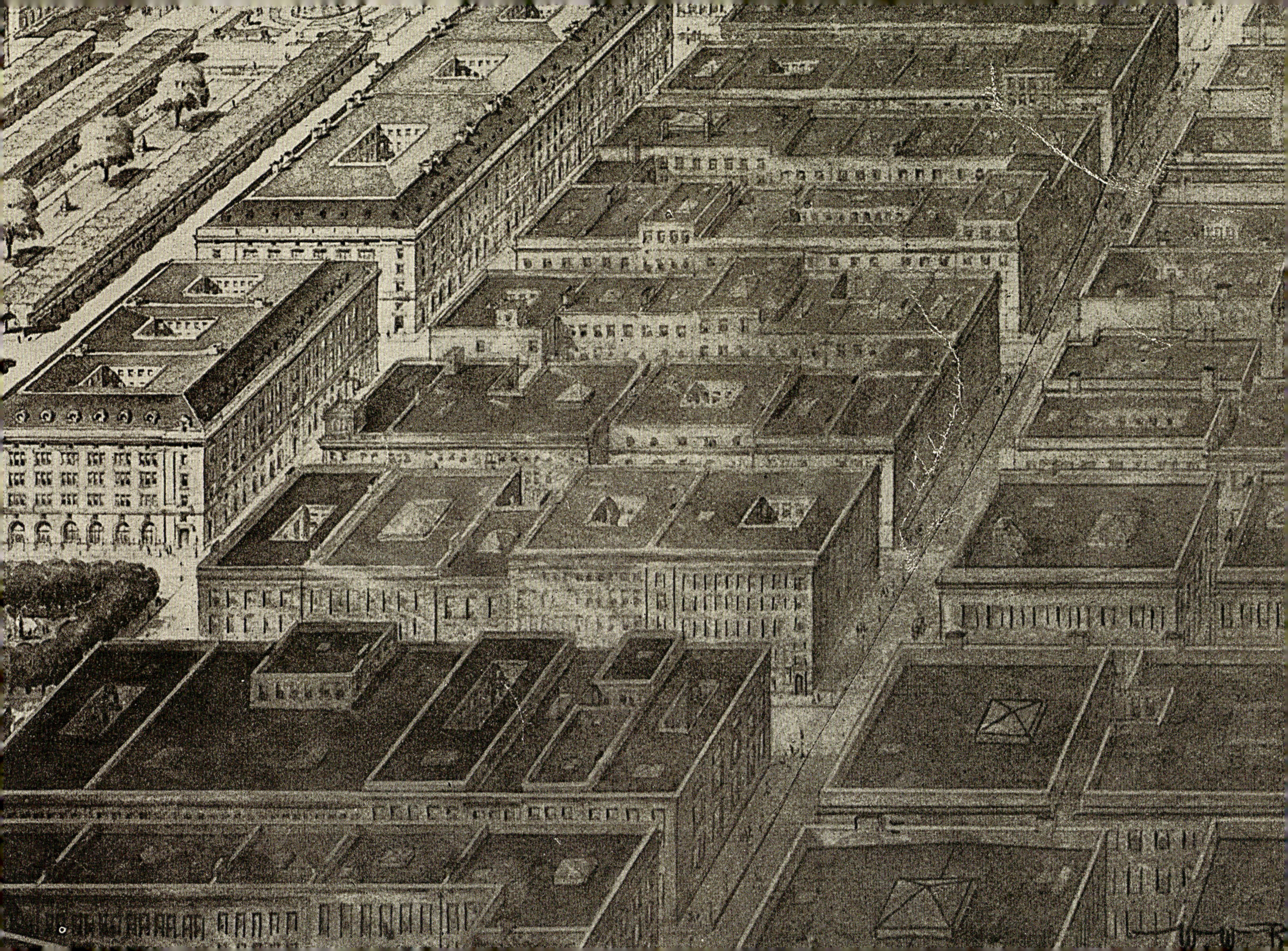

Plate 41 – Garrett Morgan The massive filtration house in what was originally the Division Avenue Water Pumping and Filtration Plant, built in 1916. Located on Cleveland's original water system built in 1856, the Garrett A. Morgan Water Treatment Plant has a capacity of 150 million gallons.

Plate 42 – Mustard Squaring off for the "Mustard Wars" are Ballpark Mustard and Stadium Mustard.

Plate 43 – Eliot Ness Ohio City's Market Tavern was established in the 1860s and served Cleveland's politicians and lawyers, including Eliot Ness, the city's law director. Today it is home to Great Lakes Brewpub, on the campus of Great Lakes Brewery, where Eliot Ness Amber Light is one of a full menu of specialty beers served. The flag in the upper right corner marks one of three bullet holes—all of them mysteries.

Plate 44 – Ohio City Franklin Boulevard showcases a collection of architectural styles popular between the late 1870s and the late 1920s, including Gothic Revival, Italianate, Second Empire, Queen Anne, Colonial Revival, Neoclassical, and Craftsman. Next door to Franklin Castle (see Plate 22) is a vacant lot, the site of a public art project, combining gardens, remains of demolished houses, statuary, and this likeness of the onion-shaped domes seen in Ohio City and Tremont.

Plate 45 – Jesse Owens Jesse Owens, Olympic Champion, 1936, by Cleveland sculptor William McVey, in 1982, stands at the southwest corner of Fort Huntington Park, near the former site of Fort Huntington, built in May 1813. In the background is Cleveland Memorial Shoreway, begun as a WPA project in the 1930s.

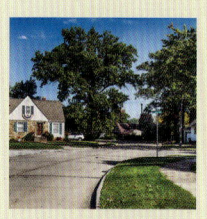

Plate 46 – Parma These blue-collar cottages stand in stark contrast to the opulent churches such as St. John the Baptist Byzantine Catholic Cathedral, St. Josaphat Ukranian Catholic Cathedral, St. Vladimir Ukranian Orthodox Cathedral, and Pokrova Ukranian Greek Catholic Church, all of which represent the varieties of ethnicities in Parma.

Plate 47 – Peerless The last "Cleveland built" was this 1932 Peerless Sedan, pictured in the Historical Society's facility on Macedonia Road where volunteers provide tender loving care to those vehicles that are not on display at the History Center in University Circle.

Plate 48 – The Perils of Society One of the rigs on a Cleveland street, waiting to be pressed into service during the filming of *Fast 8*, the latest in the series of *Fast and Furious* films shot on the streets of Cleveland.

Plate 49 – Anna Perkins Although the Crawford Auto-Aviation Museum is nationally recognized, of equal importance is the Historical Society's Chisholm Halle Costume and Textile Collection, one of the largest such collections in the nation. Pictured is Newspaper Annie's outfit, part of the collection, matched with a period hat.

Plate 50 – Pierogies In the kitchen of Seven Roses, a Polish restaurant in Cleveland's Slavic Village, where specialties include stuffed cabbage rolls, pork schnitzel, sweet peppers and chicken, kielbasa, saurkraut, potato pancakes, and pierogies.

Plate 51 – Pittsburgh The one-time Pittsburgh Road first traces the east side of the Flats and then cuts south to face the steel mills in the Flats head-on. The intersection ahead could be called the Confluence of Oil and Steel. Turn right on Rockefeller Avenue, and just over half a mile ahead, at the intersection of Rockefeller Avenue and Transport Road, is the site where Standard Oil Refinery #1 once stood.

Plate 52 – Polka A display at the National Cleveland-Style Polka Hall of Fame and Museum celebrates "America's Polka King," accordionist Frankie Yankovic. Yankovic released more than 200 recordings in his career and was the first musician ever to receive the Grammy Award for the Best Polka Recording.

Plate 53 – Public Square A grand ceremony marked the opening of the transformed Public Square in time for the Republican National Convention in 1936. Features of the Square include Concert Hill, the green space to the north, and the Splash Zone and the Rebol Café to the south. The entire space is tied together by walking paths. The first formal event was a belated Fourth of July concert by the Cleveland Orchestra.

Plate 54 – Thomas Quayle Ship building is alive and well in Cleveland. This tugboat is under construction at Great Lakes Shipyard, a subsidiary of the Great Lakes Group, for delivery to Guatemala. Great Lakes Towing Company was founded in 1899, and among the founding shareholders were John D. Rockefeller and Jeptha H. Wade.

Plate 55 – John D. Rockefeller Known for giving dimes to strangers, John D. Rockefeller is buried at Lake View Cemetery, where visitors to his graveside leave dimes in return. The family plot at Lake View Cemetery, marked by an imposing obelisk, is otherwise simple, keeping with the understatement that was preferred by the man who created such immense wealth.

Plate 56 – Shaker Heights A site of many "firsts." First it was the site of the Center Family of the North Union Society of Shakers (1822–89), and then the site of the first Shaker Heights Village School (1912–14), and later the Shaker Heights Village Hall (1911–31).

Plate 57 – Belle Sherwin This period display in Cleveland's History Center is a tribute to the role of progressive women in Cleveland and one of Cleveland's most famous progressives, who went on to a position of national leadership. Belle and her kindred sister, Anna Perkins (see Plate 49), were agents of change, each in her own way.

Plate 58 – The Shoreway Approaching downtown on the Shoreway from the east, drivers are faced with a choice. Choose the right lanes where the Shoreway continues through Cleveland to Lakewood, or the left lanes to negotiate the sometimes trecherous Dead Man's Curve and follow I-90 or access I-71 or I-77. At rush hour, traffic can be backed up for miles going through the curve, but at other times, unsuspecting truckers who enter the curve at highway speed may find their vehicles flipped on their side.

Plate 59 – Short Vincent Street One of the attractions on Short Vincent was the Theatrical Restaurant, where entertainers, politicians, and mobsters alike, could be seen elbow to elbow at the bar. Established in 1937, the Theatrical burned to the ground in 1960. It was rebuilt and reopened the following year. While the facade remains, and one can clearly see where the letters spelling out the Theatrical's name were affixed, the building is now a parking garage for workers and visitors to the bank and office towers that replaced one of Cleveland's hottest spots.

Plate 60 – Slavic Village Amid the old-world architecture that has always been associated with Slavic Village, new development is breathing fresh life into the cluster of neighborhoods that were so hard hit as the epicenter of the subprime mortgage crisis of 2008 and the Great Recession that followed.

Plate 61 – SOM Center Road The one place at which we understand the origin of the name is at the intersection of SOM Center and Wilson Mills Roads where traces of Mayfield Center, including this gazebo and the Center School (1906) can be seen.

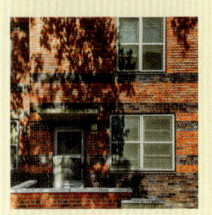

Plate 62 – Stokes The Stokes brothers grew up at 4301 Case Court in one of the city's first federally funded housing projects, Outhwaite Homes. Carl became the first African American mayor of a major American city, while Louis became the first African American congressman from the state of Ohio.

Plate 63 – *Time* Magazine The view from the window of the great American photographer Margaret Bourke-White's office and adjacent darkroom on the twelfth floor of Cleveland's Terminal Tower. Now obstructed in part by the Tower City's Skylight Office Tower, it was through this window that Bourke-White made one of her many photographs of Cleveland's industrial Flats.

Plate 64 – University Circle Sponsored by the Cleveland Museum of Art, the annual Parade the Circle has brought cultural and community organizations together in University Circle since 1990. More than 1,200 participants and 80,000 spectators, a variety of food trucks, and games and activities combine to make Parade the Circle one of Cleveland's summer highlights.

Plate 65 – The Vans Twelve stories above the hubbub of Cleveland Union Terminal in its heyday was the Van Sweringen brothers' Greenbrier Suite, consisting of the Great Hall, an orchestra balcony, a boardroom, a kitchen, and dining room. The thirteenth and fourteenth floors were the brothers' private quarters, where they sometimes spent the night instead of going home to their mansion in Shaker Heights, or their country estate, Daisy Hill.

Plate 66 – Vinegar Hill In 1894, Vinegar Hill became home to a steam plant, providing heat and steam power to meet the growing needs of the commercial district of the city. In 1993, a second facility was brought online to provide chilled water to its customers in downtown Cleveland. Today, Cleveland Thermal is converting its boilers from coal to natural gas in order to reduce its carbon footprint.

Plate 67 – Wade Lake View Cemetery is the final resting place of Jeptha Homer Wade who died in 1891. The monument is situated on a bluff with a commanding view of the cemetery, the city, and Lake Erie, surrounded by the graves of generations of Wade family members. Down the hill, on the bank of Wade Pond, stands the Wade Memorial Chapel, replete with interior walls and a window from the studio of Louis Comfort Tiffany.

Plate 68 – Western Reserve/Connecticut Western Reserve This replica of the home of Lorenzo Carter, Cleveland's first permanent resident, was commissioned by the Cleveland Women's City Club in 1976. Carter arrived in the Western Reserve in May 1797 and was joined by his wife, Rebecca, and their nine children. He traded fur with the Indians, farmed, and operated an inn and tavern, which served as a town hall.

Plate 69 – Whiskey Island The manual shovel and bucket process of unloading lake freighters was revolutionized in 1880 with the introduction of the Cantilever Crane, invented by Clevelanders Fayette Brown and his son, Ephraim. Automation took another big step at the turn of the century with the introduction of the Hulett Unloaders. Invented in 1898 and built by another Clevelander, George Hulett, the unloaders scooped the cargo out of the freighter's hold and discharged it directly into railcars for delivery to the mill. These Huletts, retired in 1998, are in storage on Whiskey Island.

Plate 70 – X Now refashioned as an R&B station, WZAK is in its new midtown location in a repurposed industrial building.

Plate 71 – Yellow Cab Company Once the staple of downtown transportation, yellow cabs have become as rare as winning football seasons in Cleveland. The NYC cab, pictured here, is poised for the shoot of a scene in *Fast 8*, the latest in the *Fast and Furious* series, shot in Cleveland in May and June 2016 (see Plate 48).

Plate 72 – Cy Young Standing at Progressive Field in this 2016 photograph are statues of pitching great Bob Feller, franchise home run leader Jim Thome, and American League color-barrier breaker Larry Doby. In 2017 statues of player-manager Lou Boudreau and manager Frank Robinson joined the grouping. Although Cy Young never wore the Tribe uniform and his likeness does not appear in among this grouping, it is undisputable that he deserves to stand with these baseball greats.

Plate 73 – The Zoo Created by Viktor Schreckengost in 1956, the mastodon and mammoth sculptures graced the Pachyderm Building at the Cleveland Metroparks Zoo. Today they stand in the Sears Garden at the entrance to University Circle, not far from where the zoo stood when it was founded. The sculptures were moved to their present location in 2016.